"What has long been a taboo topic between employer and employee, and an often angst ridden journey for expectant mothers and employers alike, now for the first time has play book. Not only that, it hits on every note. You need not look any further for how to handle a maternity leave."

Carolyn Lawrence, *Leader, Gender Diversity and Inclusion, Deloitte Canada*

"After reading through Making It Work! I wish I could have read this before I went through my own maternity leaves a few years ago. It's a well-researched, well written guide for women taking maternity leave. In our workplace at ATB Financial, we directly consider diversity and inclusion of team members. The guidebook explicitly considers what maternity leave might be like for diverse groups of women."

Michelle Beck, *VP People & Culture, ATB Financial*

Making It Work!

How to effectively navigate maternity leave career transitions

— AN EMPLOYEE'S GUIDE —

Avra Davidoff, Laura Hambley, April Dyrda, Julie Choi,
Colleen Lucas, Rebecca Teebay-Webb, Michelle Cook

ceric
CANADIAN EDUCATION AND RESEARCH INSTITUTE FOR COUNSELLING
INSTITUT CANADIEN D'ÉDUCATION ET DE RECHERCHE EN ORIENTATION

Canada Career Counselling
Connecting the pieces

Making it Work!
Copyright 2016 by Avra Davidoff, Laura Hambley, April Dyrda,
Julie Choi, Colleen Lucas, Rebecca Teebay-Webb, Michelle Cook

Editor: Sheryl Khanna

Wholesale discounts for book orders are
available through Ingram Distributors.

Tellwell Talent
www.tellwell.ca

Published by:
Canadian Education and Research Institute for Counselling
(CERIC)
2 St Clair Avenue East, Suite 300
Toronto, Ontario
M4T 2T5
Canada
website: www.ceric.ca
Email: admin@ceric.ca

ISBN
Paperback: 978-1-988066-14-1
EBook: 978-1-988066-15-8

Contents

Acknowledgements i

Project Team iii

Introduction 1

    Purpose and Potential 2

Making it Work!
A Canadian Perspective 3

    Demographics 3

    Key Themes 5

    Areas for Improvement 7

Mothers in the Modern Workplace
The Business Case 11

    Knowing Your Value in the Workplace 12

    Rebranding:
    Understanding Your Professional Potential as a Mother 13

    Communicating Your Value 16

Modern Maternity Leave
Career Development, Progression,
and Advancement Defined 19

    One Solution - Moving from the Ladder to the Lattice 20

    Knowing Your Career Style(s) 21

Careers in Process 23

    Understanding You 23

Beliefs of Working Mothers...25

Other Career Considerations..25

Elevating Your Career Development...31

Information interviews...31

S.M.A.R.T. career goals...32

Interview like a S.T.A.R..32

Social Media Tips for Working Mothers...33

Understanding Change and Transition...37

Understanding Modern Working Mothers......................................39

Disclosing Pregnancy: Fears and Apprehensions.......................39

Moods and Motherhood...41

Striving for Excellence: The Push-Pull of Work and Home.......42

From Myth to Reality: Overcoming Working Mother Myths.......43

Understanding Modern Employers...47

Before The Maternity Leave Transition..51

Accommodations at Work..52

Career Dialogues...53

Preparing for the Transition..55

Pre-Maternity Leave Exit Interview...56

Return to Work Plan..57

During the Maternity Leave..61

Enact and Revise the Communication Plan...................................61

Return to Work Logistics..63

Confident Competence...64

Comeback Coaching...66

Combatting the Imposter Syndrome...67

Post-Maternity Leave/Reintegration...77

Return to Work Interview..78

Mentorship and Sponsorship..78

Customizing Your Career
Alternative/Flexible Work Arrangements

Customizing Your Career
Alternative/Flexible Work Arrangements *81*

How to Approach the Topic of Flexible Work 82

Telework and WORKshift 83

Job-sharing 86

Flexible hours 88

Part-time work 89

Mompreneurs 93

Considerations for Diverse Populations 99

First-Time Mothers Under Age Twenty-Five 100

First-Time Mothers Over Age Forty 101

Adoptive Parents 102

New Immigrant Mothers 102

Aboriginal Mothers 103

Same-Sex Mothers 103

Five Working Mother Mantras 105

Conclusion 106

Glossary 107

Endnotes 115

Acknowledgements

This project was funded by the Canadian Education and Research Institute of Counselling (CERIC), who we thank for enthusiastically recognizing the need for this project. We would also like to thank the research and content development team at Canada Career Counselling, whose career and life experiences, as well as passion for career development, are infectious and inspiring. In addition, we would also like to thank the many employees and employers from across Canada, who provided valuable insights and feedback through focus groups, surveys, and interviews. And finally, to all of our community partners and organizations who supported and promoted this project from development to dissemination, we thank you for helping to make a difference for mothers in Canada and the organizations who employ them.

Project Team

Avra Davidoff - Project Lead, Researcher, Content Developer

Avra Davidoff is a workplace psychologist, and Associate at Canada Career Counselling and the Leadership Success Group. She currently practices in the areas of career development, leadership development, and diversity. Avra holds a Master's in Counselling Psychology, with a career counselling specialization, from the Graduate Centre for Applied Psychology at Athabasca University.

Dr. Laura Hambley - Project Advisor, Researcher, Content Developer

Dr. Laura Hambley founded Canada Career Counselling and has worked in the field of career development since 2001. Laura holds a Master's in Applied Psychology and a PhD in Industrial/Organizational Psychology from the University of Calgary. As an Adjunct Professor of Psychology, Laura regularly contributes to research in career development.

April Dyrda - Research Assistant, Content Developer

April Dyrda is pursuing her Master's in Counselling Psychology at the University of Calgary. She currently works as a practicum counsellor at Mount Royal University and serves as a student mentor through the Canadian Psychological Association and the University of Calgary. Her research is based on the career development of post-secondary students.

Julie Choi - Research Assistant, Content Developer

Julie Choi is an Industrial/Organizational Psychology Consultant with a broad range of skills. Julie received her MSc in Industrial/Organizational Psychology from the University of Calgary in 2014, and is currently completing her PhD with a focus on understanding the factors that influence how a subordinate views their leaders.

Dr. Colleen Lucas - Researcher, Content Developer

Dr. Colleen Lucas holds a PhD in Industrial/Organizational Psychology from the University of Calgary. She lives in Calgary and practices in the areas of career counselling, and leadership assessment and development. Her research interests include psychological contract violation in the workplace, organizational learning and change, and career and leadership development.

Rebecca Teebay-Webb - Researcher, Content Developer

Rebecca Teebay-Webb is a Registered Provisional Psychologist with the College of Alberta Psychologists. She practices in the areas of career, personal, and trauma counselling, and works with both adults and adolescents. Rebecca holds a Master's in Counselling Psychology from Yorkville University, and a BSc from the University of Liverpool.

Michelle Cook - Content Developer

Michelle Cook has a passion for coaching and assisting clients to achieve career satisfaction. She specializes in career planning, post-secondary education, and professional branding through powerful resumes, cover letters, networking, and interview coaching. Michelle holds a BA in Psychology from the University of Calgary and is a working towards her Certified Career Development Practitioner designation.

Dr. Stephanie Paquet - Researcher

Dr. Stephanie Paquet is a Senior Associate Consultant with Knightsbridge Leadership Solutions in Calgary. She has consulted with organizations in a variety of industries in the area of talent management, including the design of selection systems, facilitation of leadership development initiatives, succession planning, leadership coaching, 360 feedback, and psychological and behavioural assessments for selection and development. Stephanie is a graduate of McGill University and holds an MSc and PhD in Industrial/Organizational Psychology from the University of Calgary.

Genevieve Hoffart - Research Assistant

Genevieve Hoffart is an MSc candidate in Industrial/Organizational Psychology at the University of Calgary, and research coordinator in the Individual and Team Performance Lab, where she manages key research partnerships. She is passionate about developing applicable tools and workshops to improve the functioning of teams in organizations across North America.

Travis Schneider - Research Assistant

Travis Schneider is an Industrial/Organizational Psychology Consultant who leverages his expertise in assessment to guide clients on their career paths. Travis holds an MSc in Industrial/Organizational Psychology from the University of Western Ontario, and is currently completing his PhD on the validity of social media for job selection.

Dr. Roberta Neault - Reviewer

Dr. Roberta Neault is an award-winning leader in career development, in Canada and internationally. Roberta is the President of Life Strategies Ltd., as well as the Associate Dean of the Faculty of Behavioural Sciences at Yorkville University. In both roles Roberta manages predominantly female faculty, staff and students, where navigating maternity leaves is an ongoing reality.

Kathleen Johnston - Reviewer

Kathleen Johnston is a Career Strategist who is passionate about facilitating women to live work in their "unique zone of genius." She is a counselling therapist, executive coach, stress consultant, career development instructor for over ten years, and contributing writer for the first Canadian colleges/universities career text. Kathleen holds a BSc from the University of Alberta and a MA in Pastoral Psychology and Counselling from St. Stephen's College.

Funding

The funding for this project was provided by the Canadian Education and Research Institute for Counselling (CERIC). CERIC is a charitable organization that advances education and research in career counselling and career development, in order to increase the economic and social well-being of Canadians.

Introduction

Welcome to *Making It Work! How to Effectively Navigate Maternity Leave Career Transitions: An Employee's Guide.* This resource was developed for women taking a **maternity leave**, which is inclusive of maternity, parental, and adoption leave, as well as any extended care and nurturing leave following the birth or adoption of a child. This guidebook is equally applicable to women who are experiencing their first or subsequent maternity leave career transition. We recognize that not every woman or her circumstances are the same and regardless of whether this is your first leave, you may experience unique challenges and opportunities in your life and your career during this time.

Certainly not exhaustive in its scope, this resource is meant to be a self-directed tool that you can use to tailor specific strategies to the needs of your situation and your career. Whether you are a stay-at-home mother or a mother in paid employment, you are a **working mother** (the term working mother will be used in this resource to refer to paid employment, volunteer, and educational pursuits).

As an **expectant mother** (either through birth or adoption) and/or working mother, it may be difficult to find relevant information to assist you with your **maternity leave career transition.** Some information may be obtained through organization policy and procedure manuals, or community and government organizations. While useful, this information is often guided by legislation versus leading and promising practices in women's career development. Legally based information is often necessary, but not sufficient in addressing the challenges and opportunities associated with a maternity leave career transition.

Our goal is to provide you with convenient and user-friendly information, which will equip you to proactively manage your maternity leave career transition. By taking the initiative to effectively manage this transition, you are setting yourself up for success. And, as Benjamin Franklin so poignantly noted, "By failing to prepare, you are preparing to fail."

We hope that by using this resource you are informed and inspired to *Make It Work!*

PURPOSE AND POTENTIAL

The information contained in this guidebook is meant to serve as a starting point to support and encourage you to develop promising career management strategies not only in navigating your maternity leave career transition, but with other career decisions you may experience in the future. We hope to empower you to become and/or maintain the role of an active agent in your career development process. In equipping you with the knowledge to manage your career effectively, we hope that you also become an agent of influence so that organizations better recognize the importance of attracting, retaining, and developing working mothers. By taking a proactive approach to managing your career, you can transfer your experiences and learnings to other decisions in your life and to other women in your networks. Our goal is that this guidebook, along with the employer version *(Making It Work! How to Effectively Manage Maternity Leave Career Transitions: An Employer's Guide)*, will help working mothers and organizations to collaboratively realize their full potential.

Making It Work!
A CANADIAN PERSPECTIVE

Between the fall of 2013 and the spring of 2015, Canada Career Counselling embarked on a mission to understand the perceptions of both **employees** and **employers** regarding the impact of maternity leave on a woman's career development. Our research team conducted focus groups, one-on-one interviews, and a national survey, which culminated in the creation of this resource, webinars for both employers and employees, and articles in various publications. Webinars will be made available through Canada Career Counselling's Website (www.canadacareercounselling.com), as well as through CERIC's Website (www.ceric.ca), in the fall of 2016.

DEMOGRAPHICS

Two focus groups were conducted with a total of ten employees working in the province of Alberta who had personal experience taking maternity leave(s). Key themes and findings from this session were used to guide interview and survey questions. One-on-one interviews were held with nineteen employees from across Canada working in the nonprofit (21%), public (63%), and private (16%) sectors. A total of four hundred and forty-one employees completed the survey portion of this research study. Surveyed employees most commonly represented the public sector (50%), as well as the private sector (27%), followed by those in nonprofit (20%), and other industries (3%).

Percentage of Participants from Represented Industries

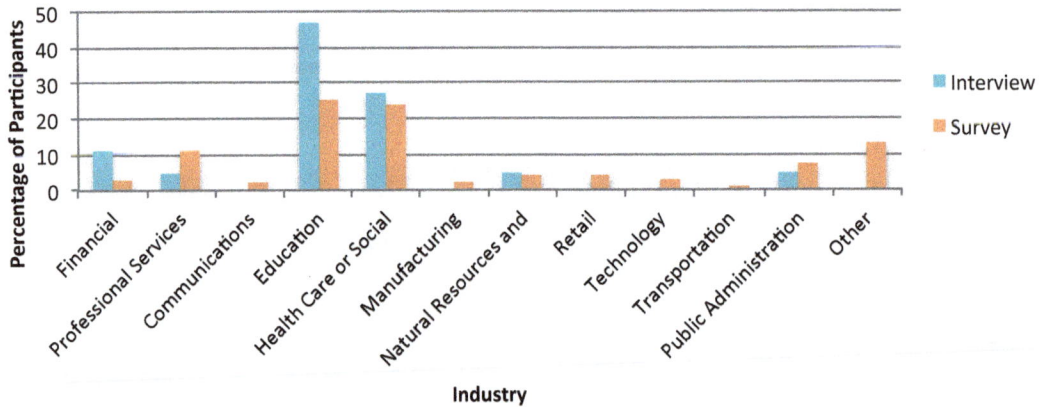

Percentage of Participants from Represented Provinces

Participants included individuals across Canada from a wide array of positions, including front-line staff (51%), middle management (30%), executives (4%), contractors (4%), and other forms of employment (11%), such as consultants, advisors, research associates, and students. Provincial representation of both interview and survey participants is outlined below.

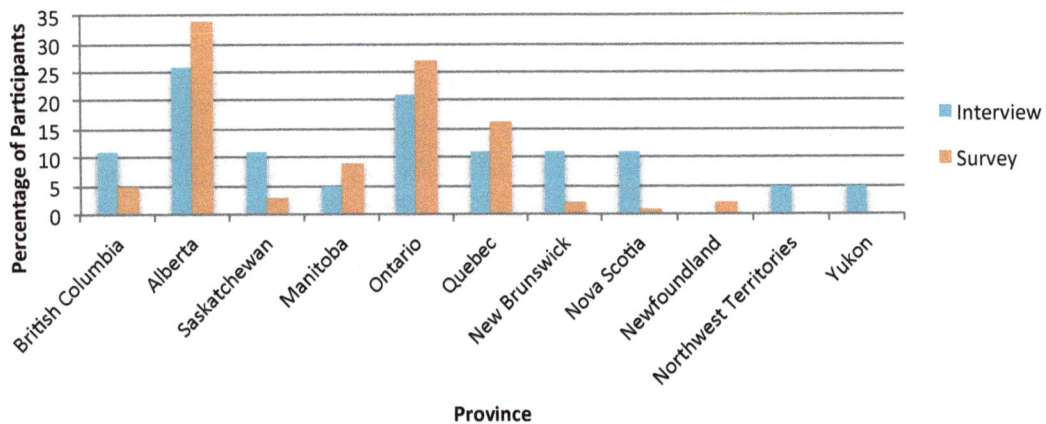

As part of the research, identifying the concerns of mothers from diverse groups was also considered important, given that they may face unique challenges throughout the maternity leave process. Five diverse groups recognized in this study were: adoptive parents (6%), first-time mothers age forty and over (28%), immigrant mothers who lived in Canada for less than five years (10%), aboriginal mothers (14%), and young mothers age twenty-five and under (18%). Additionally, 46% of surveyed mothers classified themselves as belonging to other diverse groups, including: single mothers, mothers with multiple children, persons with disabilities, a visible ethnic or racial minority group, and same-gendered couples.

Percentage of Participants from Diverse Groups

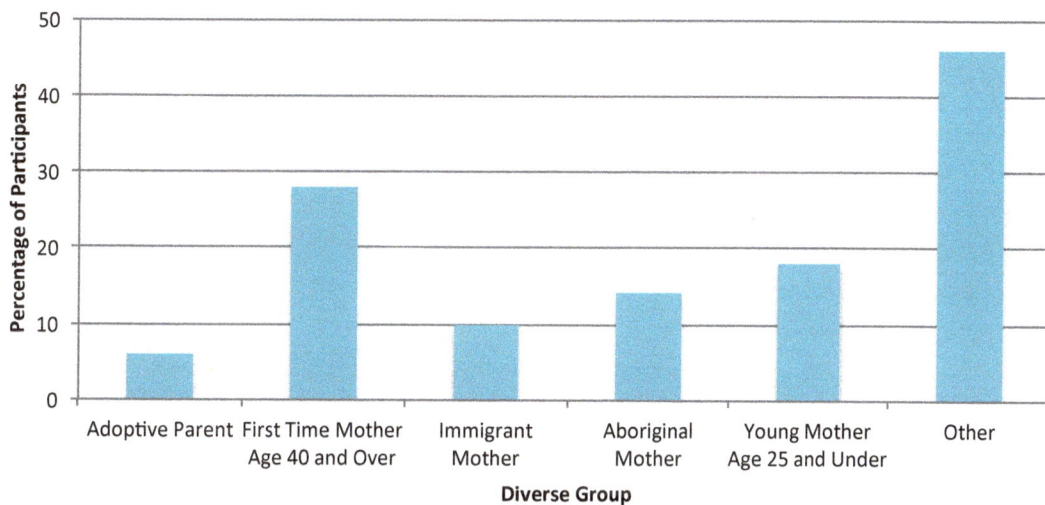

KEY THEMES

Mothers who participated in our research study indicated that the most valuable thing an organization can do for new and expectant mothers is to normalize the maternity leave process. Understanding maternity leave to be a normal part of many employees' lives helps remove the stigma associated with this leave.

"We need to consider [maternity] leave as a bigger concept, instead of just focusing on it being the woman's issue. This will allow for a wider acceptance and normalization of the process. Only then can we truly focus on what a maternity leave actually means."
- Employer Quote

While 60% of the women in our study had taken a maternity leave of ten to twelve months, only 27% of those surveyed had partners who had also taken some form of parental or paternity leave during this time. Among those with partners who also took leave, an overwhelming majority (81%) had only taken one to three months off from work.

Months of Leave Taken From Work

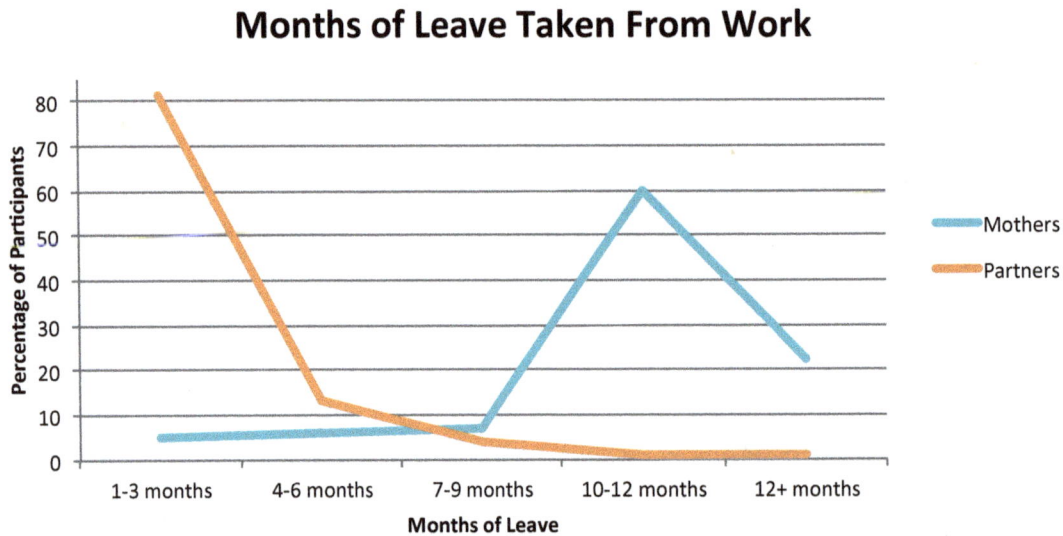

The vast majority of surveyed employers (85%) felt that maternity leave had either a neutral or positive impact on the career development of their employees. However, a significant number of new mothers (36%) felt that taking maternity leave had negatively impacted their opportunity for promotions, career development, and career progression, with less than 4% indicating that maternity leave had positively impacted their career. This may be due in part to the fact that the majority of mothers surveyed (51%) felt that maternity leaves were not managed well overall.

Surveyed mothers were also asked to reflect on the impact that maternity leave had on their career orientation, including their desire to be on a leadership track, the amount of energy they had for work, and personal investment in their work role. While most mothers indicated their maternity leave had a neutral impact on their work (46%), many indicated that they felt less engaged and less effective at work after having children (37%).

51%

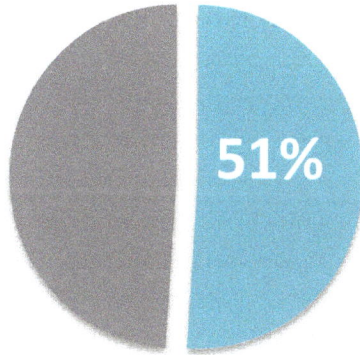

51% of surveyed mothers felt that maternity leaves were managed **less than well** by their workplace. An additional 28% and 21% indicated that maternity leaves were managed **well** and **very well**, respectively.

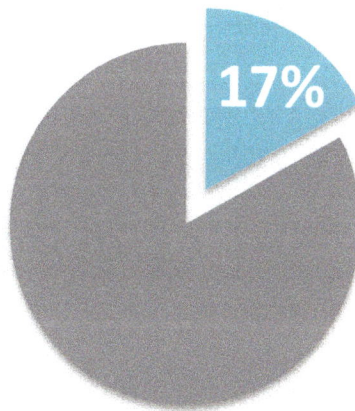

17%

17% of surveyed mothers indicated that taking a maternity leave had a **positive impact** on their effectiveness at work, increasing their work engagement and career-orientation.

AREAS FOR IMPROVEMENT

In many organizations and for many new mothers, the maternity leave process can be a confusing and uncertain time. One interviewee noted, "There is not a lot offered to employees or their employers to prepare them for the maternity leave." Survey respondents and interviewees consistently indicated that it is often left up to the employee to manage her maternity leave, with the organization being unwilling or unable to offer support and guidance.

Below we have identified areas for improvement to assist you in managing your maternity leave transition process. These and other suggestions are discussed in detail throughout the guidebook. The findings and recommendations have been divided into three phases: before, during, and after the maternity leave. Each phase has its own distinctions and thinking about your maternity leave and the focus on each stage will help you apply strategies at various phases.

Before the Maternity Leave

Communicate your needs: Some women require additional accommodations at work during their pregnancy in order to maintain the health and safety of both themselves and their child. In the months leading up to your maternity leave you have a legal right to ask for temporary accommodations at work as well as a responsibility to explain to your employer exactly what kind of help and assistance you require. These modifications may be physical, environmental, or in regards to greater flexibility to your work schedule.

Discuss your transition: Review each of your expectations, including how the organization can better support you as a working mother, and whether you have all of the necessary resources to be successful in your position before leaving and upon returning to work. Having this conversation with your employer prior to your maternity leave also allows each of you to ask any questions and/or express any concerns.

Establish a communication plan: In collaboration with your employer, determine how much communication you feel would be appropriate while you are on maternity leave. Have a conversation about how often updates will be given, and how communication will be maintained (e.g., telephone, e-mail, text, mail, or in person).

During the Maternity Leave

Engage in professional and/or personal development: Although your maternity leave may be a time when your job is put on pause, you may still want to engage in professional and/or personal development. Whether it is taking part in a training seminar, attending a workshop or event, or simply meeting with friends or colleagues, connecting with other like-minded individuals during your leave can help increase your competence and confidence.

Maintain the communication plan: Although your employer should be responsible for upholding the established **communication plan**, this plan generally allows for two-way communication that invites you to periodically check in with your employer or colleagues to discuss work and other topics. If you find that the established communication plan is no longer feasible, do not hesitate to discuss possible revisions with your employer.

After the Maternity Leave

Have a return to work interview with your employer: When you choose to return to work there may be a number of changes to your work circumstances as well as other aspects of the workplace. Having an open dialogue about any changes in roles and responsibilities with your employer will allow both of you to clearly communicate and negotiate expectations.

Take part in a re-onboarding process: After being on maternity leave it can sometimes be difficult to reintegrate into the workplace. Be sure to discuss with your employer the possibility for **re-onboarding** and re-integration, not only into your work role, but also into the social environment of the office.

Discuss flexible work arrangements: Whether you gradually return to work or implement other **flexible work arrangements**, the opportunity to have flexibility in your work creates room for integration between work and family lives. As a mother returning to work, better **work-life integration** allows you to be more effective in both your role as a parent and as an employee. Consider what flexible arrangements may suit you and have a conversation with your employer about what options are available in your workplace.

"There are still huge opportunities for employers to be more attractive to working mothers. Support is often found in pockets or subcultures of an organization, but the acceptance of having children as being a part of life needs to be more widespread." - Employer Quote

Mothers in the Modern Workplace
THE BUSINESS CASE

What is it about maternity leave that carries negative connotations for some? When considering other types of leaves, such as a **medical leave**, the same stigma does not seem to apply. Additionally, when taking a medical leave, employees often leave with limited notice and their return date is uncertain, unlike in the case of a maternity leave. It is important that as a mother, you set any negative inferences aside and encourage those in your work environment to do the same. Working mothers are major contributors in the workplace, and organizations reap numerous benefits from supporting rather than stigmatizing working mothers.

"People need to treat maternity leave like any other type of leave. If we just changed our language and the way we talked about this type of leave, then it wouldn't be such a unique or female-only situation. If organizations didn't make such a big deal of mat leave and knew how to handle the transition better, it wouldn't be viewed so negatively. It's a leave, and it happens to coincide with the birth of a child, but it's not different from any other type of leave." - Employer Quote

Women make up approximately 50% of Canada's labour force and account for 58% of post-secondary graduates.[1] The employment rate for working mothers has increased steadily over the last three decades, and 73% of mothers report working in either a part-time or full-time capacity.[2] Working mothers are a significant component of the labour force, and it is important for you to recognize what you have to offer, and leverage your strengths.

According to a research study conducted by global workplace provider *Regus*, over a quarter of businesses globally are planning to hire more returning mothers in 2015 compared to 2014, and for good reason.[3] In their New York Times Best Seller, *Womenomics*, Claire Shipman and Katty Kay suggest that having women in strategic positions within an organization can increase organizational profitability.[4] In support of this claim, researchers at *Catalyst*, a leading North American nonprofit research and advocacy organization dedicated to the advancement of women in the workplace, compared the financial performance of organizations that had more women in leadership positions to organizations with no or fewer women on their boards. It was found that the former outperformed the latter in the following ways:[5]

- Return on equity by 53%

- Return on sales by 42%

- Return on invested capital by 66%

So, why does the strategic placement of women in the workforce have such a strong influence on the bottom line? When women are enabled to work effectively at all levels of the organization, there is a noted increase in organizational creativity and innovation, improved customer understanding, and enriched corporate social practices.[6]

"If organizations just switched their approach and philosophy on maternity leave they would be able to reap the rewards." - Employer Quote

---

When presenting and communicating your value to your employer there are a number of practical benefits you should highlight that come from supporting new mothers in their return to the workplace. These include:

Retained talent: As a mother who has chosen to continue to work after maternity leave, chances are that you will be well versed in the demands of your work role. From the perspective of your employer, this can save the organization a great deal of time and money by retaining the skills and talent you offer. Although this may come at a marginal cost, training a new employee would cost the organization substantially more (e.g., the costs associated with recruitment, advertising, and training) than reintegrating someone who is already familiar with the role.

Reduced turnover and hiring costs: Improving recruitment and retention is critical for all organizations given the high cost of replacing employees, including recruitment, onboarding, and training. A recent study found the average cost of replacing employees to be approximately 40% of the annual salary for entry-level staff, 150% for mid-level employees, and up to 400% percent for specialized or high-level employees.[7]

Improved morale and commitment: Many mothers express an increased likelihood of returning to work if they believe their organization is committed to them. This means that employers who demonstrate their commitment to you leading up to and while on maternity leave are more likely to receive that same level of commitment back upon your return, a reciprocity of care that other staff members also tend to pick up on. When an employer demonstrates this level of commitment to their staff, levels of morale, loyalty, and engagement tend to improve across the organization, which ultimately increases levels of performance and productivity.

As both a woman and an employee returning to work following a maternity leave, there are numerous benefits and business opportunities that you have to offer. Understanding that your return to work is not only beneficial for you, but also for your employer is the first step in realizing the potential and value that you bring. However, you may be wondering what benefits, if any, there are to being a *mother* in the workplace. Is there any specific or added value that you bring to your work because you have a child? The short answer to this question is, absolutely! In the next section, we've outlined some of the workplace advantages of being a mother and how you can effectively communicate to your employer all you have to offer.

REBRANDING:
UNDERSTANDING YOUR PROFESSIONAL POTENTIAL AS A MOTHER

In her book, *Grow Your Value: Living and Working to Your Full Potential,* Mika Brzezinski writes about the experiences of successful women, including her own, and breaks down what it means to fully express your value as both a woman and a mother in the workplace.[8] Her book focuses on the importance of rebranding yourself and how this can easily be done during career transitions. According to Brzezinski, **rebranding** involves not only understanding what you have to offer an employer, but also using it to your advantage by sending out a strong, positive message. When you are able to do this, being a mother no longer remains stigmatizing or problematic...it becomes empowering.

When you return to work following a maternity leave it can sometimes feel like the label of "mother" is printed across your forehead. Rather than viewed around the workplace as a colleague or a co-worker, your status as a mother can quickly come to the forefront. Being a mother often comes with other labels, such as "tired" or "preoccupied," which may not reflect well on or accurately represent your ability to be present and effective at work.

However, as a mother you are encouraged to consider ways in which your family life can be an opportunity for rebranding at work. In an interview with *Working Mother*, an American-based magazine for career-committed mothers, Brzezinski states "all those [labels] that can come into the room with you can be useful, as long as you put them in their place. That stuff is useful, a badge of honor."[9]

So what exactly do you have to offer as a working mother? In what way do these new labels bring added value to your work? In her interview with *Working Mother*, Brzezinski suggested that to answer these questions, women should stop and take inventory of both their professional value and their inner or personal value. She encourages women to write these values down and take a clear-eyed look at what they already have. Use the following table to write down and reflect on some of the value or skill that you have to offer both professionally and personally:

Professional Value	Personal Value
Characteristics you possess that you consider valuable at work and in your career.	*Characteristics you possess that you consider valuable in all other areas of your life (e.g., as a mother, a partner, a friend).*
1. Organized	1. Supportive
2.	2.
3.	3.
4.	4.
5.	5.

In looking at the list you have created, you will probably notice that many of the characteristics you identified as valuable in your personal life are also relevant and applicable to your professional life. As a mother there are a number of characteristics you already possess that will make you more desirable in the workplace. In fact, working mothers tend to excel in the following areas that are highly valued by employers:

Dependability: As a mother, you likely make every effort to be available for your family when you are needed, and this same commitment tends to be reflected in the workplace. While there is a common misconception that having a child detracts from a mother's ability to be present at work, this tends not to be the case. In fact, mothers are often well equipped to adapt quickly to changing circumstances, and will do so in order to meet and exceed workplace demands. In a study conducted by J. A. Kmec, it was found that mothers were just as reliable at work in terms of their effort on the job compared to both fathers and employees without children.[10]

Efficiency: New mothers develop and fine-tune a number of skills during the maternity leave process, notably their level of efficiency. When returning to work this efficiency tends to carry over, such that mothers have been found to work more intensely on the job compared to women without children.[11]

Productivity: Research shows that while new mothers tend to work less hours than before they had children, they are just as effective and productive in their jobs when at work.[12] All employees, not just those with children, are likely to produce higher quality work at the office when they are able to commit time to their lives outside of work. While it may seem counterintuitive at first, employees who are able to spend quality time at home tend to be more productive at work, as they are likely to reciprocate that high level of quality when in the office.

Task and time management: Having children tends to turn even the most disorganized of us into all-star task managers, which is relevant at home and in the workplace. Skills that are valued on the job, such as focus, organization, and time management, are often enhanced through the experience of being a parent. In fact, when a mother has work responsibilities added to responsibilities at home, her ability to manage time and prioritize work may become enhanced.

Having and raising children demands a great deal from you, but it also serves as a chance for learning and growth. Rather than a period of time taken out of your career, it can be helpful to view your maternity leave as an opportunity for the development of skills that will support you as both a mother and an employee when and if you decide to make the transition back to work.

COMMUNICATING YOUR VALUE

Knowing that you are a valuable asset to an organization is one thing, but effectively communicating this to your employer is another. You may recognize how much you add to the organization, but does your manager/supervisor recognize this? According to Katty Kay and Clair Shipman, authors of *The Confidence Code: The Science and Art of Self-Assurance – What Women Should Know*, women are naturally less comfortable than men at promoting themselves, dominating conversations, and speaking to their accomplishments, particularly in the work environment.[13] Fortunately, there are more subtle ways of communicating your value that will allow you to sell yourself without the need to boast:

Act as if you can: It is common after returning from a maternity leave to feel a lack of confidence in yourself and your ability to perform in the workplace, even if this perception is unjustified. However, you can do a lot more than you give yourself credit for. You have probably heard the phrase, "fake it 'til you make it," and this is the same concept as "acting as if you can." If you do not feel like you add value to your workplace, act like you are someone who does. Believe it or not, one of the best ways to build competence, success, and fulfillment in your life is simply by changing your attitude and *acting* more confident. By spending less time worrying about whether you are competent and more time focused on self-belief and action, you will not only become more confident, but also more competent.

Be valuable: A big part of communicating your value is *being* valuable. If you are an asset to your organization, your value will be showcased in the work that you produce. At times, we can get caught up in our work schedules and seclude ourselves, falling into the background. To avoid this, have regular conversations with your employer about what your priorities on the job should be, and focus your time and energy on these goals and tasks. Making a conscious effort to connect with your manager/supervisor to discuss the work that you are doing not only ensures that you are maximizing your productivity, but also ensures your contributions are being communicated to your employer.

Speak to your accomplishments: As much as you would like them to, sometimes your accomplishments do not speak for themselves. Oftentimes the work that you do becomes expected, routine, or somehow falls between the cracks. To ensure that your employer recognizes what you have put into a project or task, make sure you deliver not only the final product, but also the results. When you accomplish a project with positive results, take the time to include those results and the ways you contributed to them in the report you give your manager/supervisor. Not only will your employer appreciate seeing the positive outcomes of your work, but it will also allow you to communicate your value without having to actually sell yourself.

Invest in your growth: Communicating your value is easier when you have more of it, and part of this involves regularly adding to your skill set. Getting involved in professional development opportunities such as conferences, workshops, webinars, or other training events will not only promote your knowledge and learning, but it will enable you to be a more active and involved member in the workplace. When you are more knowledgeable about the work that you do, you will naturally have more to offer. In rapidly changing industries, such as technology and research and development, it is especially important to stay on the cutting edge. Maximizing your professional development will allow you to contribute innovative, creative, and productive ideas to meetings as well as the work that you do, which is something your employer can recognize and appreciate.

Modern Maternity Leave
CAREER DEVELOPMENT, PROGRESSION, AND ADVANCEMENT DEFINED

It is important to have a clear definition of some of the keywords being used in this guidebook so that you can move your self and your career in the direction that makes the most sense for you. The following keywords are defined in the Glossary, but we wanted to go into greater detail here with a few career-related keywords and examples.

Career is the sum of all the paid and unpaid roles a person has held in their lifetime, and **career development** is the ongoing acquisition or refinement of knowledge, skills, and abilities. **Career progression**, or career advancement, refers to the movement towards a particular career goal(s), the achievement of which may or may not include a change in title, responsibility, status, pay, flexibility, influence, or other factors which are determined as important and worthy of pursuit. Note the implication of this definition, that progression and advancement are non-directional (title, pay, or responsibility may increase or decrease), developmental in nature, and individually defined.

For example, a consultant or entrepreneur may hold the same title for the majority of their career, but may advance her skill set, expertise, customer base, and revenues as her career progresses. A working mother may also have different definitions of progress and advancement to correspond to different career and life circumstances. We often accept traditional notions of career progression and advancement, such as vertical movement and increase in pay, but there is some risk in using a one-dimensional ruler to measure the multiple facets of your career. Assuming that the only measure of career advancement is to move up in an organization is a limiting view to adopt.

Given that organizations are much flatter, that people transition within and between industries at quicker rates than did previous generations, and that we have observed an increase in entrepreneurial and contract workers, our understanding of progression and advancement must also shift in response to these trends. If not, you risk adapting others' ideas of success rather than integrating and developing your own version of success.

ONE SOLUTION - MOVING FROM THE LADDER TO THE LATTICE

Adopting a modern take on career progression is one step you can take to address the previously noted concerns. While many are familiar with the metaphor of the career ladder, it is a concept that is quickly being replaced with the career lattice. While the **career ladder** characterizes career progression as a vertical movement, the **career lattice** conceptualizes career progression in more than one direction and can include horizontal, vertical, downward, and diagonal movement. The career lattice is responsive to the individual's life circumstance (e.g., family or health status) as well as external factors influencing career development (e.g., the economy or existing opportunities within the organization), and promotes the collaboration and customization of careers and the structure of work. The career lattice encourages the continued growth of the organization and the employee by creating a variety of, and valuing *all*, career paths.

Ladder progression

Lattice pathways

Examples of linear
career paths

Examples of more varied
paths for growth and
development

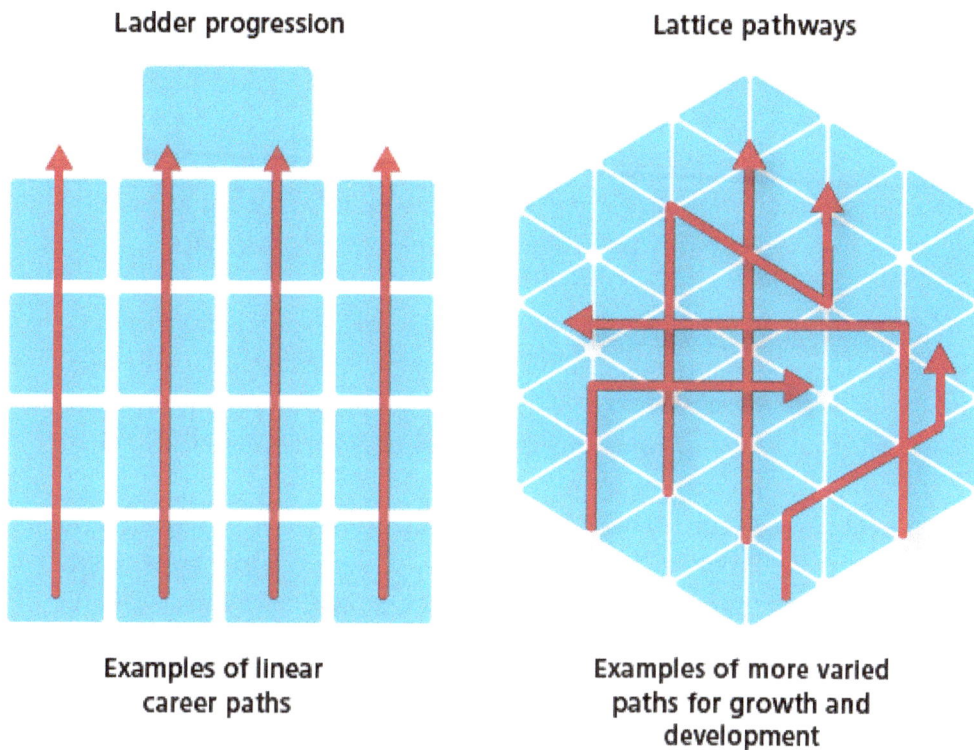

KNOWING YOUR CAREER STYLE(S)

With organizations becoming flatter and with the increase in workforce diversity, there is a broader range in how individuals are defining career success. The basis for this definition often stems from each individual's beliefs and values. While it is normal for you to compare yourself and your career to the experiences of others, this may have a negative impact on your career and self-esteem if you do not understand that different career experiences and values can and do exist.

In *Career View Concepts: Roadmaps for Career Success*, Brousseau and Driver suggest that career concepts can be summarized by three fundamental differences:[15]

Stability - Should my career change or stay the way it is?

Direction - In what direction should my career go (e.g., upward, lateral, downshifting)?

Duration - How often should I make career changes?

Depending on how you answer the above questions, Brousseau and Driver developed four **career concepts** to account for how people view careers.

The **Expert Career Concept** is the most common and traditional conceptualization of career. It emphasizes the lifelong commitment to one profession, and mastering knowledge and skills in a particular field. Individuals with this career concept often value commitment, quality, security, and specialization.

The **Linear Career Concept** emphasizes upward movement consistent with the idea of the career ladder. This concept is characterized by an increased level of responsibility, influence, and status. Individuals with this career concept typically value leadership, competitiveness, and achievement.

The **Spiral Career Concept** is much less traditional and is characterized by lateral change, typically every five to ten years. Individuals with this career concept tend to develop a much broader skill set. Each transition builds upon existing skills. The term spiral illustrates how career evolves, spiralling outward from a core set of knowledge, skills, and abilities, with the application of these attributes to new environments. Individuals with this career concept typically value variety and personal growth.

The **Transitory Career Concept** is the least conventional of the concepts and is characterized by the most change. Others may not even view this pattern as a career. A person with this concept consistently seeks change. Individuals with this career concept typically value variety, independence, and flexibility. These people often work as contractors due to these values.

As a mother, you may adopt one, several, or all of the career concepts over the course of your career to reflect the changes in your circumstances and within you. You may also choose to combine more than one concept at the same time (e.g., expert and spiral) to describe the style of career that you would most like to achieve or that best suits your circumstances.

Careers in Process

Much like your role of being a mother, your career is also a unique process that is developmental in nature. While we have previously outlined some new ways of thinking about your career, it is also important to understand the pieces of you that influence your maternity leave career transition.

"As moms we have multiple responsibilities and need flexibility to meet the demands of them. It's important to have constant dialogue about one's work load and capacity to do it, never in comparison to other co-workers." - Employee Quote

UNDERSTANDING YOU

Taken from Calgary Career Counselling's workbook, *Connecting the Pieces: A Workbook for Creating Your Ideal Career*, you will find some of the key components of career decision making in the following diagram.[16] It is important to recognize that some of the components will change over time in response to experiences you have, while others remain fairly constant. For example, you can always develop new interests, but aspects of your personality may remain consistent throughout your life.

Interests/Passions - A particular thing/subject/content area to which a person is drawn. Passions are extreme interests and are often accompanied by strong emotional attraction.

Personality - The unique combination of your emotional, attitudinal, and behavioural patterns.

Reality - Situation and circumstances that impact your career options. Reality changes the options we consider, and results in different opportunities and limitations.

Skills/Abilities - Refers to learned skills/abilities that can be enhanced through practice and increasing one's knowledge related to the particular ability. Two main types of skills include transferable skills and job specific or technical skills.

Values - Refers to things that you consider to be important to you. These are the things in our life that keep us feeling happy and/or motivated.

Beliefs - Strongly held convictions or ideas.

As with other transitions and experiences in your life, a maternity leave career transition can impact all of the factors noted above and some may have a more pronounced impact on the career decisions you make. For example, you may be willing to sacrifice some interests in exchange for a flexible work schedule.

BELIEFS OF WORKING MOTHERS

We gain messages about work, careers, and being a mother from a young age. These beliefs and ideas shape our expectations about our career and ourselves. This information can come from parents, other family members, friends, our culture, and the media, just to name a few sources. It is important to examine these beliefs and understand how they may help or hinder you in effectively managing your maternity leave career transition. For example, you may have been told that specific careers are better for women, or that mothers should not work outside the home.

Messages Regarding Your Career and Your Role as a Mother

Use the table below to organize your beliefs. First, identify the belief you have or messages you have received about your career and/or your role as a mother. Then try to determine if that belief has had a positive or negative impact on your career.

Belief	Impact
Being a teacher is a good profession for a mother	Negative impact; limits my perceived career options

OTHER CAREER CONSIDERATIONS

As intentionally highlighted throughout this resource, your maternity leave career transition is unique to you, although others may share some commonalities. In this section we explore some other considerations, which may continue to uniquely impact you and your career.

The concept of the **employment contract** (sometimes referred to as the "psychological contract") began to surface in the early 1990s. The employment contract is an unwritten contract outlining the roles, responsibilities, and expectations of the involved parties, typically between the employer and employee.

Under the **old employment contract**, employees were often guaranteed lifelong employment in exchange for loyalty. Under the **new employment contract**, employees are guaranteed employment only as long as they continue to add value to the organization. Also under the new employment contract, either party can terminate the contract at any time if one party determines they are no longer benefitting from the relationship, or when the costs outweigh the benefits. For example, an employee may terminate the contract when he or she no longer feels challenged or valued.

Expectations of the old employment contract still influence how individuals make career decisions. This is especially true for individuals who entered the labour market under the era of the old employment contract, but who are now working under the new employment contract. As many individuals and organizations are unaware of the new employment contract's existence, numerous organizations and individuals continue to be in flux, caught in transition between the old and new paradigm. For example, many organizations encourage their employees to continue to develop and add value to the organization but typically reward employees based on longevity versus performance.

Below is a summary of the key elements of the old and new employment contracts:[17]

Old Contract	New Contract
Job Security	Employability
Credentials/Degrees	Continuous Learning
Entitlement	Adding Value
Job Title	Portfolio of Skills
Success - Career Ladder	Success = Individually Defined
Reliance on the Organization	Individual Responsibility

Given the previous descriptions of the old and new employment contract, it is important for you to reflect on what type of organization will meet your needs as a working mother, and how best to prepare yourself for the psychological contract at said organization.

Dual-Career Partnerships

It is increasingly common for both partners in a relationship to have paid jobs outside the home. In Canada, the number of dual-income families has steadily increased over time. In 2014, 69% of husband-wife families with at least one child under the age of sixteen reported being dual-earners, which is up from 36% in 1976.[18] A **dual-career partnership** can be a choice and sometimes an economic necessity. In these situations, one partner's career can impact the other's, and often requires some discussion and compromise about how best to manage each person's career.

According to Neault and Pickerell, many dual-career relationships report experiencing challenges related to:[19]

Role conflicts: Demands imposed by one role conflict with the demands of another role (e.g., careers versus family responsibilities).

Household responsibilities: Managing household activities, such as cooking, cleaning, and household supports (e.g., housekeepers, childcare providers).

Finances: Feeling as though one or both partners could not afford to earn less.

Time: Insufficient time for self (including hobbies and wellness activities), family, friends, or simply taking time to be present and pay attention.

Dual-Career Success Strategies

If left unchecked these dual-career partnership challenges can result in negative impacts for both personal and career roles. In the following section, Neault and Pickerell outline some suggestions to address the previously noted challenges.[20]

Home and Family Interventions

· **Relationship building:** Communicating more effectively, understanding and being responsive to a partner's needs, and facilitating mutual encouragement, support, and adaptability.

· **Financial management:** Examining financial commitments and prioritizing spending.

Personal Well-being Interventions

· **Work-life integration:** Identifying an appropriate and realistic mix of life-work roles.

- **Stress management:** Identifying positive and negative stress factors and developing positive coping strategies that support the development of resiliency.

- **Time management:** Re-evaluating priorities and scheduling time accordingly, and exploring time management tips and strategies.

- **Wellness:** Making decisions that support a healthy lifestyle, including getting enough sleep, exercise, and eating nutritious food.

Career Interventions

- **Career counselling:** Exploring alternative and sustainable careers including work that may be less demanding, more flexible, or pays more for less hours (e.g., consulting).

The above strategies can help you address and deal with dual-career pressure points. Although the list certainly is not exhaustive, you may want to consider connecting with relevant professionals, other working mothers, and organizations in your community to explore additional ideas.

Multiple Career Households

To alleviate the financial costs associated with parenthood, and/or to seek additional support, the traditional home structure is shifting. Multiple income earners living under one roof can be just as common as traditional dual-career families. Working mothers may not only cohabitate with a partner, but may live with their parents, other family members, or friends for a variety of reasons. Hence, **multiple career households** may be the norm.

Braverman states that for a variety of reasons, multi-generational housing, or the propensity for multiple generations to live under one roof, is becoming more and more common.[21] In 2013, more than half of home buyers who were older than fifty-five claimed that they preferred a home with an in-law suite, which is up 28% from 2007.[22] Working mothers may move back in with family and friends after starting families of their own. Common reasons why these arrangements are increasing is for cost sharing purposes, given rising home prices and stagnant wages, debt level, an end of a relationship, cultural preference, or caregiving responsibilities as in the case of providing care for an elderly parent.[23]

Making Working Households Work

Living in a multiple career household can also incite a set of additional responsibilities that may need to be negotiated and require compromise. This may involve taking care of parents, and elders, or perhaps having additional children to care for while other caregivers are working.

In entering this type of arrangement you may want to think about and, if appropriate, discuss the following:

· Your reasoning or motivation to enter into this type of living arrangement.

· Your short-term and long-term goals.

· The action steps to achieve your goals and an exit strategy should the situation not work out.

· Division of labour around the household.

· Boundaries you and others may benefit from setting.

· How bills and household expenses will be managed between parties.

· How the careers of others will impact your career and vice versa.

Portfolio Careers

The way we define work is continually evolving. For instance, work no longer refers to the traditional 9:00 to 5:00, and women (and men) may choose to hold multiple jobs for a variety of reasons. This can come in the form of working a part-time job, volunteering, **multi-tracking** (i.e., holding more than one paid role at the same time), or participating in experiential learning opportunities. The percentage of women holding multiple jobs continues to increase, and in 2009 about 56% of multiple job holders were women, which takes up 6.2% of all employed women.[24] Indeed, some reasons a working mother may pursue multiple careers at the same time or over the course of their lifetime include motivators associated with finances, interest, values (e.g., challenge), or labour market.

Some estimates suggest individuals will experience between five to ten career changes over their working life. People experience career change and transition for a number of reasons, including both external factors (e.g., termination, lay-off, accident, illness) and internal factors (e.g., choice, interest). For this reason, it is increasingly likely that individuals develop **portfolio careers**, a range of knowledge, skills, and experience that can be applied in new settings. It is not uncommon for employed mothers to develop portfolio careers in response to maternity leave career transitions as they pursue opportunities that correspond to circumstances (e.g., need for flexibility) versus a specific career target.

Career Evolution

Much as your behaviours and interactions change to correspond to the age and stage of your child, your career too requires similar adaptation. Career is developmental in nature; it is not a "once and done" style of decision making. The importance of your career relative to other aspects of your life may change over time. It is important to reflect on, and identify how, your maternity leave career transition impacts your priorities. Adapt your goals and objectives accordingly and take actions that support what makes sense for you.

Elevating Your Career Development

At some point during your maternity leave career transition, you may find yourself looking at the possibility of exploring a new position, either within or outside your current or last place of employment. This section will provide you with some practical information and strategies to plan and prepare for this opportunity.

INFORMATION INTERVIEWS

An **information interview** is a meeting initiated by you with someone in a career or industry you are interested in. The goal is to further understand the role or industry and gain information and advice to help you decide if it is truly a direction you want to pursue. Although it may seem anxiety provoking to meet with someone you do not know, it is one of the best ways to learn about a career and industry beyond what you are able to find out from job postings. People are often willing to meet with you, especially if they like what they do. And, do not be afraid to put your networks to work, including your social networks, like LinkedIn. Once you let other people know that you are considering a career move, someone you know may be able to connect you with an individual in that particular career whom you can then interview.

One way to achieve your career targets is to plan out the change you want to make by creating a set of goals. Keep in mind that goals are not meant to be rigid (they can change). You may be reluctant to modify your goals as doing so could be perceived as failure, but rigidly adhering to goals that are no longer meaningful to you can result in frustration, stress, and a waste of resources including time and money. Changing goals is an important part of adapting to your circumstances; therefore, it is necessary to adopt a flexible approach to goal setting. The following is a great framework for setting goals:

- **Specific**: Be specific about what you want to achieve.

- **Measurable**: How will you know you achieved your goal, and by what means can you measure or determine your progress?

- **Achievable**: Can the goal be achieved?

- **Relevant**: Is it the right goal at the right time for you?

- **Time Sensitive**: Put a time frame on it so you know you are accountable to the goal.

Example of a vague goal: I want to network more.

Example of a smart goal: I would like to have coffee with four senior marketing professionals in the next five months.

INTERVIEW LIKE A S.T.A.R.

If you are like most opportunity seekers, the thought of an interview can be nerve wracking, especially if you are not sufficiently prepared. Having a model to prepare and structure your interview responses can ease your pre-interview anxiety. Many organizations use behavioural-based interviewing practices based on the **S.T.A.R. approach**, which assumes your past behaviours will be a good predictor of future behaviours. As an example, a typical question may include, "Tell me about a time you had to deal with a very angry customer." The following example shows you how to answer this question using the S.T.A.R. approach:

1. Begin by describing the *situation* or *task*: "In my current position I received a complaint from a very angry customer who was upset that her product was not received on time and was damaged upon receipt."

2. Then describe your *action* to respond to the situation: "I remained calm and assured the customer I was interested in helping her to resolve the issue. I told her that I would get to the bottom of this but first I needed to gather additional information. I then asked her a few more questions to better understand the situation and how I might be able to assist her."

3. Note the *result* of the situation: "I was able to identify an error in the online ordering process which explained why the item was late and I also learned that the item was not inspected by the warehouse staff prior to packing, which may have explained the damage. I communicated the error in the online ordering process, which was fixed and we also instituted a process around inspecting goods before packaging."

4. To elevate your response to the next level, you can conclude by noting the skills you used in this situation: "To successfully resolve this situation, I had to use effective customer service, problem solving, as well as communication and negotiation skills."

If interviewing is something you struggle with, consider getting the support of a career counsellor or job search strategist to help develop and fine-tune these important skills.

SOCIAL MEDIA TIPS FOR WORKING MOTHERS

Using **social media** can be vital to your potential job search and career development in general. Research shows a continual increase in social recruiting, where recruiters take advantage of social media to find qualified candidates. The most popular site is LinkedIn, followed by Facebook and Twitter. However, if you are going to invest your time into social media for career development and job search, LinkedIn is a must as it is currently the go-to for recruitment and is considered the most professional site. You may also find other social media platforms useful, depending on your career goals.

Importance of Social Media

- Allow potential employers to learn about your work history, education, and industry knowledge (facts to back up your resume), and the attitudes you express publicly.

- Allow you to stay relevant in your industry. You can follow people who are industry experts or mentors, and groups that promote knowledge sharing on new trends and topics. Are there relevant topics or articles that you can share in group forums? The more you interact with your network and followers, providing valuable contributions, the more you increase your chances of being discovered by a recruiter.

Tips for Leveraging LinkedIn

- Create a strong profile, using content and keywords that are industry specific and highlight your areas of expertise, skills, and abilities; what words would you use to find someone with your skillset? Do a search on LinkedIn and take a look at some of the profiles of people who are using those words to get ideas and strategies about how to market yourself.

- Write a creative tagline. Rather than your current or past job title, use words that will help recruiters find you.

- Write your profile in first person and showcase your creativity and personality. If applicable, include links to work you have done, articles you have written, projects you have worked on, media mentions, etc.

- If you are currently on maternity leave, leave your tagline and organization the same as when you were employed, as you are technically still employed. It is not necessary for anyone to know you are on leave as it may prevent interested parties from approaching you by assuming you are not interested in exploring opportunities at the time. Being on a maternity leave is also better explained in an interview rather than through an online profile.

- If you have left employment to care for your child, change your tagline as noted in the second bullet and leave your current employment blank. Avoid providing information that may lead others to make inaccurate assumptions. Think carefully about using a tagline indicating you are a stay-at-home mom. It is not anyone's business what you have been doing and it is not an indication of your ability to do a job.

- Are you currently volunteering? This is valuable information that you can add to your profile. Do not undervalue the skills you are developing in volunteer roles and list them like you would in your paid positions.

Tips for Leveraging Facebook and Twitter

- One of the biggest pitfalls with Facebook and Twitter is people's tendency to over share and post content that may not be appropriate. Be cautious with your posts, as there is potential for employers to dismiss you if they see your content as unfavourable.

- As with LinkedIn, follow companies you are interested in as potential employers. This is a great way to find out what is important to the company and allows you the opportunity to align yourself with their interests, corporate mission, and/or values.

· Connect with and follow professionals in your industry of interest. More than 70% of jobs are landed through knowing someone in the field, so growing your network increases your chance of finding employment.[25]

Understanding Change and Transition

A new addition to the family can lead to significant changes in your home life and your work life. Everyone handles change differently and some of the changes you experience will be unique to your situation. However, by understanding the transition period leading up to your maternity leave, during your leave, and transitioning back to work after your leave, you can gain a better understanding of the challenges and opportunities you may face during this time.

"So much of how a maternity leave unfolds depends on the individual manager, no matter how good or supportive the policies are. Your experience depends on the support you have at work. Everyone's maternity leave is different." - Employer Quote

Bridges' Model of Transition

A helpful model to conceptualize the maternity leave transition has been developed by William Bridges.[26] Bridges made an important distinction between *change* and *transition*. *Change* is situational—the baby or adopted child is coming and you will be away from work for a period of time. The *transition* is psychological—it is a three-phase process that you go through as you internalize and come to terms with the details of the new situation that the change brings about. This includes your new expanded family, potentially not being as involved with the business of work, and/or returning to different work arrangements after your leave.

Bridges' three-phase process includes the ending, the neutral zone, and the new beginning. Although it may seem counterintuitive, transition begins with

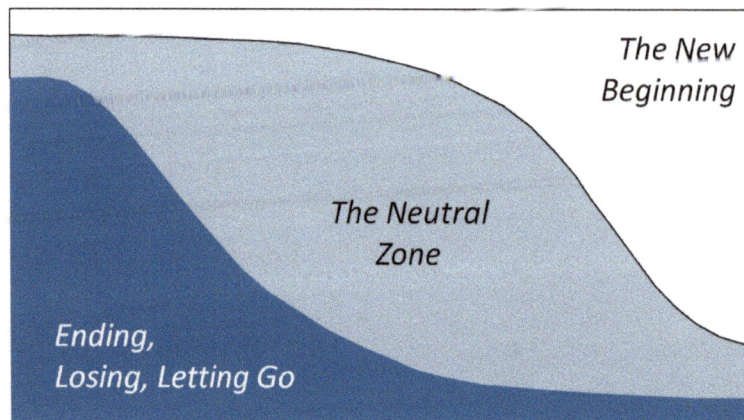

an ending. The *ending phase* corresponds to the time before you begin your leave and before the baby arrives. During this time, you may feel excited and apprehensive about how well you will adjust. It is important to accept and acknowledge these emotions; talking with someone who has gone through a similar experience can help normalize your experience.

The *neutral zone* corresponds to the time when you are on leave. During this time, you will be adjusting to changes in your routine and home life, and may or may not be involved in work related activities. You may feel anxious about being out of the loop and not knowing what is happening at work. If you would like ongoing communication, it is a good idea to talk to your employer prior to your leave and develop a communication plan to ensure that you are informed of any changes at work, possible training opportunities, etc. Unless you have agreed to it, your organization cannot contact you during your leave.

After the maternity leave, your transition back into the workplace represents the third phase, the *new beginning*. You may be experiencing mixed emotions at this time, excited about returning to work but anxious about leaving the baby. There may also be changes at work. For example, you may be coming back to a new position, new colleagues, new working arrangements, and/or new processes on which to be trained. Working with your employer to create a step-by-step plan for your reintegration can alleviate the anxiety you may be experiencing and ensure a smooth transition.

Understanding Modern Working Mothers

As a new or expectant mother, you may be experiencing a wide range of emotions and feelings. Many expectant mothers describe feelings of happiness, excitement, and amazement. However, you may also be feeling anxious and experiencing or anticipating struggles prior to maternity leave, during maternity leave, and/or upon return to work post-maternity leave. You are not alone! This period can be transformational for many women, and along with this transformation it is common to experience a variety of emotions, feelings, celebrations, and struggles.

DISCLOSING PREGNANCY: FEARS AND APPREHENSIONS

Not every mother-to-be has fears or apprehensions about disclosing her pregnancy or plans to adopt; it largely depends on her workplace and the nature of her relationships with her manager/supervisor and co-workers. Having concerns about disclosing your plans to your employer is not uncommon. For example, you may fear that your employer will view you as less focused on your role, and on your long-term career overall. You may also have concerns about your employer and colleagues treating you differently.

Other common concerns include the loss of responsibilities or commitments within the usual scope of your work role, as they are re-assigned to other colleagues in anticipation of your maternity leave. That is, you may fear that others will view you as a short-term contributor rather than a long-term asset within the organization, especially if they assume that you will not return to work post-maternity leave.

Some expectant mothers notice a growing sense of gradual invisibility, shifting from someone who was once valued within the organization, to someone unessential. The transition towards motherhood can create feelings of insecurity in a mother who perceives, accurately or mistakenly, that she is being excluded from long-term decision making within the workplace.

"At best, I felt that I had returned to a placeholder position with an empty title, but certainly not as the contributing, valued member of the team I had been previously and was eager to be again." - Employee Quote

Expectations and Anticipation

Upon your return to work following maternity leave, feelings of anxiety, insecurity, and a lack of confidence may still be present. You may assume that your colleagues view you as a less productive member of the team due to your new responsibilities at home. As a mother, you may also be dealing with internal pressures if you feel the pull between home and work life. Your desire to be a "good" mother could potentially compete with your professional desire to regain your status as a valued, respected employee with a viable future within the organization.

It is important to recognize that working mothers experience a wide range of emotions leading up to, during, and after a maternity leave; often experiencing different emotions with each subsequent leave. Regardless of what feelings you experience, this guidebook will provide some practical tips and strategies to support you through your maternity leave career transition.

"During my pregnancy any discussion about my maternity leave or plans for what would happen when the baby arrived caused severe anxiety. I did everything in my power to hide my pregnancy from co-workers and my supervisor for as long as possible. I just didn't want to talk about it." - Employee Quote

Feeling Valued and Being Appreciated

Returning to work can be tough, but if you feel supported by your colleagues, have the opportunity to connect with others who have also experienced maternity leave career transitions, and have an opportunity to share your experiences openly, you may experience lower levels of anxiety upon returning to work.

Such opportunities can also increase feelings of inclusion at work, allowing you to experience a renewed sense of belonging.

"Communication while the employee is on maternity leave is key to having them return. Otherwise, employees will feel disengaged and may choose to look for employment elsewhere." - Employee Quote

MOODS AND MOTHERHOOD

The arrival of a new baby is exhilarating and exhausting. It can be a challenging time and can affect you both physically and emotionally. Not surprisingly, these changes can be overwhelming. This may result in the **baby blues**. Experiencing the baby blues is normal and affects some mothers during the first few weeks following childbirth, at which point the symptoms typically lessen and diminish. During these times, mothers may experience mood changes consisting of happiness and joy that can quickly turn to feelings of depression and sadness. Other symptoms can include irritability, restlessness, insomnia, anxiety, fatigue, poor concentration, and impatience.

If you experience the baby blues, lean on others and engage your support system, such as your partner, family members, friends, doctor, a counsellor, or community members for support, reassurance, and assistance. Reaching out for professional support services that provide non-judgmental counselling can also be helpful (i.e., psychologists, social workers, and other counsellors who specialize in helping new mothers).

Postpartum Depression and Mood Disorders

If you find that the symptoms of the baby blues do not diminish after two weeks, or if your symptoms worsen, you may be experiencing a **postpartum mood disorder** (PPMD). If your symptoms are concerning (e.g., hopelessness, sleep disturbance not related to the baby, feelings of harming yourself), seek professional help for support and a professional evaluation. PPMDs include **postpartum depression** (PPD), postpartum anxiety, postpartum obsessive compulsive disorder, postpartum post-traumatic stress disorder, postpartum bipolar II disorder, and postpartum psychosis.

PPD is the most common complication of childbirth.[27] Symptoms may begin during pregnancy for 10% to 16% of women diagnosed with PPD; for other women symptoms begin right after and up to a year following childbirth. PPD not only affects first-time mothers, but mothers who have given birth in the past, and adoptive mothers.[28]

Whether you are experiencing baby blues, PPD, or challenges in general, services such as professional counselling, and your family doctor, can support you.

STRIVING FOR EXCELLENCE: THE PUSH-PULL OF WORK AND HOME

Motherhood can be profoundly transformative and life changing for women. As a consequence, you may feel internal pressure related to being a "good mother" and a "good employee" simultaneously. You may also experience dual anxiety stemming from the pressure to return to work and the guilt and unease related to your child attending childcare while you are working.

Individually, the roles of mother and employee can be highly demanding. It can understandably feel overwhelming when you have both home and work responsibilities to attend to, especially if you experience internal and external pressures to be in both places, and to manage both roles expertly. In trying to meet competing demands, you could experience a psychological struggle as you reconcile both your paid work role and your new role as a mother. However, the drive or need to achieve both can be significant. You may be driven to return to work due to a strong desire to continue growing and developing in your career, or perhaps there is a financial need or motivational desire to contribute to your household income.

No matter the reason(s) you have for returning to work, being in the workplace does not have to take away from being a mother, and vice versa.

"There is very strong pressure in our society to work as much as possible. This puts parents of young children at a distinct disadvantage in the workforce, particularly when it comes to career advancement." - Employee Quote

In North America there are certain expectations about the ideal worker; these employees work long hours, are willing to sacrifice their personal lives for their work, and are constantly "connected."[29] This ideal persists in light of the fact that now, more than ever, employees place great value on work-life integration. Additionally, the belief that time and performance are related comes with little merit.[30] Yet, when working women become mothers, there is an outdated belief that they will be less-than-ideal employees due to changes in the amount of time they are able to devote to their employer and their career.

Many people confuse the fundamental reason why working mothers are stigmatized. People commonly believe that *children* are the reason why mothers cannot be successful post-maternity leave when, in fact, a penalty is assessed on mothers who work because they violate workplace norms (i.e., the perception of an "ideal worker") and social norms (i.e., childbearing, housework). This **motherhood penalty** is a form of prejudice that holds women back and prevents organizations from allowing these employees to maximize their potential. Organizations should be held accountable to create a culture that acknowledges working mothers as competent and fully capable. What can you do to facilitate this cultural acceptance and perhaps actively engage in a way that maximizes your potential to be a successful employee? The first step is to address, head on, the myths that surround working mothers. The following sections provide suggestions on how working mothers can confront and debunk such myths.

"What's frustrating is I feel like I am being punished for trying to be a successful, career-oriented woman." - Employee Quote

Myth # 1: Women cannot progress in the workplace once they have had a child

Studies show that women can unintentionally hold themselves back in the workplace.[31] In fact, while conducting focus groups with working mothers, Mattam and Seth identified that women wait longer before submitting applications for advancement, are less likely to leave their comfort zone in a professional setting, and will not spend as much time creating informal networks that can help with professional development.[32] Despite successes, women may also suffer from imposter syndrome, where they feel that they do not deserve their current role and that someone will be able to identify that they do not belong in that role. It is, without a doubt, unrealistic for women to be able to juggle both home and work responsibilities without support, so working mothers should take advantage of the resources that are available to them.

Organizations are beginning to provide progressive alternatives for individuals beyond just flextime. For instance, some organizations have programs that focus on personal branding, networking, career self-management, and leadership essentials. Working mothers should actively seek out these alternatives, and if they do not exist, seek support and guidance to create them for yourself!

Myth #2: Creating work-life integration is not feasible for mothers working outside the home

Women may feel that they are being stigmatized for shouldering an almost impossible set of responsibilities. Indeed, many mothers working outside the home find it challenging to integrate their roles, with over 40% claiming that family roles interfere with work roles.[33] However, mothers readily make adjustments by putting more effort into working better and harder, and sacrificing leisure time.

Mothers are often aware of the biases that exist, and for fear of letting their family responsibilities become publicized at work, they take extra care to integrate their responsibilities. This is actually beneficial to employers, given that mothers learn work-relevant skills such as multitasking, focus, organization, and creativity.[34] Working mothers need to recognize that although this mentality may be beneficial for employers, there are ways to buffer the limited time a working mother may have. You do not need to be dependent on others; you can compromise and provide trade-offs (i.e., if you can pick up my child from school, I will take your child to soccer on the weekend). Know that your workload will ebb and flow, and be ready for those accommodations by seeking help when necessary. Ensuring you have these responsibilities in order will allow you to focus on your work, rather than worry about your home responsibilities.

"I value my time so much more now. When I am at work, I am happy to have the mental space of my own and to contribute to something of value outside the home. When I am at home, I am so thankful to be there." - Employee Quote

Myth #3: Working mothers are not as competent as working fathers

Can a woman succeed at both home and work duties? Depending on who you ask, the answer to this question can range from a solid "yes" to a fervent "no."[35]

When Kmec asked employees to identify how much effort they put into their workday, there was no difference in mothers' reported work effort compared to fathers and childless workers.[36] In fact, mothers are more likely to report that their responsibilities at home do not reduce the effort put in at work. Sadly, however, the success of working mothers is often held to stricter performance standards than their male counterparts.[37]

One way to optimize your workday is to stop feeling guilty about choosing to work, and prioritize your responsibilities, depending on what comes up.

An extremely valuable resource to address potential challenges is to find a support system within your organization or industry. This support system works best when the supports you seek are in similar professional and personal life situations to your own, rather than exclusively from the C-Suite (i.e., CEO, COO). This mentor-peer group provides an opportunity for women to connect with others and learn how to face challenges and achieve goals both in the office and at home.[38]

Myth #4: Children are better equipped for life when a stay-at-home mom raises them

This issue has been a central debate for years – which choice is better for *your child?* There are arguments for and against both positions. One can reason that when a mother is able to spend more time with her child, she has control over how the child is raised and what the child is exposed to. These mothers are also purportedly capable of building stronger bonds with their children. Despite the negative media images and social stigmatization of dual-earner parents, research shows that many of these families are thriving.[39] Additionally, most families report that they are successful in managing their myriad of responsibilities.[40] In fact, the little impact that maternal employment has on children, which is generally positive, depends on other factors.[41] When children are able to form multiple attachments when their mother is not around they are able to flourish, and in a high quality childcare setting, they can develop improved language skills, social/emotional abilities, and have fewer behavioural issues.[42] Although mothers need to decide what is right for them, they should do so without fear of repercussion. There are both pros and cons for working outside of the home while raising a child; however, it is worth noting that no adverse impact is observed in child development when the proper measures are taken.

As a mother, there are many things that need to be considered when deciding when, how, and if you want to reintegrate into the workplace. Ultimately, it is your choice, but when you are dedicated to both working and parenting, the biggest issue is to overcome **psychological barriers.** Psychological barriers come in many forms including fear and mistrust, and are thought patterns that perpetuate a belief that you cannot accomplish something. You are more than capable of juggling both responsibilities and performing well in both situations, and you have the research to back it! It may take some time, and it will not be an easy road, but it is possible, so do not let social stigmas determine your success.

"I had experienced multiple instances where superiors, colleagues, work associates and friends had made decisions for me about what I can and cannot do based on the fact that I have a 'young family.' I find these assumptions very oppressive." - Employee Quote

Understanding Modern Employers

The employee and the employer have certain responsibilities before, during, and after a maternity leave. What steps does the law require and what steps are courtesies? Under the *Canadian Human Rights Act*, it is illegal for an employer to fire, mistreat, or refuse to hire a woman because she is pregnant.[43] However, as an employee, there are also legal requirements that must be taken to facilitate your maternity leave transition.

It is important to note that the below points are not comprehensive or exhaustive and will not apply equally to all mothers across Canada. It is important to review the laws for your province/territory since legislation can be unique to each region and may have changed since this publication was released.

1. You must provide your employer with written notice of your leave. Some provinces have time requirements to satisfy this notification.[44] For instance, in Alberta, you must give at least six weeks of written notice advising your employer of the date you intend to start your leave.[45]

    1.1 By law, your employer is allowed to request a written medical notice to certify the pregnancy and the due date.

    1.2 While six weeks may seem like a long notification period, it is often better for employers to receive more notice, if possible. This will allow the employer to better prepare for the upcoming transition.

    1.2.1 Although in some cases, like adoption, you may not be able to provide your employer with notice of your leave far in advance, be mindful and ensure that you provide information as it becomes available.

2. If notice cannot be given earlier (e.g., some adoption cases, premature labour, medical complications), the latest that the employee can notify their employer of their intent to take maternity leave is two weeks prior to her last day of work, and she must provide a medical certificate.[46]

3. Employees who intend to share parental leave with their partner (up to fifty-two weeks depending on the province) must inform their respective employers of their intentions. The minimum required notification period can shift depending on geographical location, so it is important to become familiar with your province/territory's legislation.

4. At least four weeks notice must be given to the employer before your expected return to work or if you would like to change your return date. An employer is not required to reinstate you until after this four week period.[47]

5. If you need an accommodation in your workplace, you are responsible for communicating this to your employer both clearly, and in a timely fashion.[48] This way, your employer can work with you to create a reasonable and accommodating solution that can help you adequately perform your role.

    5.1 When you need an accommodation, it is your responsibility to provide your employer with adequate medical information. In some cases, you may be required to follow-up with your doctor to provide your employer with more information.[49] Your employer must remove any threats to your pregnancy by making the necessary changes in your job duties and/or work area.

    5.2 Given that pregnancy places unique demands on women, employers may make special concessions to address these physical and psychological needs or demands. In some cases, your employer may give you another position within your organization or, if the organization cannot adjust your work to create a safe working environment, you may be offered special leave. You may receive financial compensation or benefits while you are on special leave.[50]

6. If you become ill and can no longer work during your pregnancy, you can take the sick leave your employer provides, which is usually compensated 100% of your normal pay. However, some small employers may not offer compensation for sick leave, in which case you may have to access medical employment insurance benefits. In some provinces, you may have job protection rights during your sick leave.

    6.1 By law, your employer can insist that you apply for employment insurance if the benefits they provide would be approximately the same amount.

7. You can consider scheduling pre-natal and other related appointments outside of work hours; however, when this is not possible, accommodation for pregnancy-related appointments cannot be withheld. This may be with or without pay, depending on the flexibility of your employer and your benefits.[51]

Additional Considerations

- An employer cannot ask about your plans to have children, your use of contraceptives, or pregnancy (even in the interview process). The extent to which they are permitted to request information pertaining to motherhood is dependent on whether the candidate can meet the assigned hours.

- Hiring decisions and promotions cannot be denied to pregnant employees, or employees who plan to become pregnant in the future.

- You do not have to take maternity leave if you do not want to. An employer must only provide you with maternity leave if you wish to take one.

- Employers should create a supportive working environment prior to the maternity leave, and doing so may require some flexibility and creativity. Some solutions can include flextime, light duties, safer duties, no overtime, etc. Some of these options are discussed in more detail in subsequent sections of this guidebook.

- Maintain an open line of communication with your employer. If you would like to work part-time during your leave, or if you would like e-mails to be sent to you throughout your leave so that you are kept in the loop, make sure to discuss these points and possible opportunities with your employer.

Before The Maternity Leave Transition

When you learn that you will soon be a mother, you may ponder, "What will my employer think?" Given the delicate nature of the subject, there is undoubtedly a time and a place to inform your employer of your pregnancy or adoption. First and foremost, you must feel comfortable about informing your employer of your plans. This may come at different points in time for each woman, especially, if pregnancy and adoption are private topics for you. Is there someone you feel comfortable disclosing the information to? You may consider reaching out to colleagues who have gone through the maternity leave process, and asking for points of contact. If there are special circumstances surrounding whom you can speak to regarding your pregnancy (i.e., only females), you should identify your options early on.

Your organization may offer you the opportunity to pair up with someone in a similar role who has already been through the maternity leave process. This person can act as an informal mentor and under this **buddy system,** can offer advice and support, as well as facilitate a smooth transition back to the workplace.

From the moment you disclose your pregnancy to your employer, there should be clear communication from both parties. Although you are required to give your employer at least six weeks notice prior to beginning your maternity leave, the more time you give to your employer, the more time you will have to adequately prepare for your departure. For instance, dealing with issues such as safety and security, accommodations in the workplace, and developing a career dialogue can only occur once the pregnancy or adoption has been disclosed.

"Maternity leave is a short period of time in the grand scheme of your employee's career. You can either damage that relationship, or truly solidify it in that time." - Employer Quote

ACCOMMODATIONS AT WORK

Unless explicitly stated by you, your employer should not assume that you are unable to perform your duties because of your pregnancy. If, however, you do require assistance, explain to your employer exactly what kind of assistance you require. If you believe your job has the potential to harm you or your baby, then you may request a workplace health and safety risk assessment. While the assessment is being conducted, you could be offered paid leave, ask for a temporary transfer to another job, or to have any potentially dangerous duties temporarily stopped.[52]

In collaboration with your employer, try and seek creative and flexible responses to your pregnancy-related needs. Accommodation ideas to consider include:

Physical/Adaptability: Strategies to meet physical demands—lifting aids, temporary reassignment of duties, reserved parking, stools, ergonomic chairs, reassignment to less physically demanding jobs, and alternate workstations.

Before you disclose your pregnancy/adoption to your employer, ensure you have explored the following:

• Your employer's practices and policies.

• Your legal rights.

• Your values and needs.

• Your goals and career aspirations.

• Your manager's likely concerns.

• Your options for flexible working.

• How and when you would like your news shared with others.

And consider the following:

• In the case of pregnancy you may want to consider disclosing sooner in case your job duties pose a risk to your, or the baby's, health.

• Come prepared with ideas and suggestions about how to manage your role and transition to and from maternity leave so it demonstrates your commitment to your job and organization.

• If you are near to a performance appraisal, consider delaying your disclosure until the appraisal is completed to ensure the news does not impact your evaluation.

• Schedule another meeting after disclosing to your employer so you can begin to work on establishing a transition plan.

Time/Flexibility: Scheduling of shifts—time off work for doctor's appointments, flexible start and end times, periodic rest, teleworking, a less physically demanding shift, limited overtime, job-sharing, and flexible use of leave.

Environmental/Individuality: Policy modifications—exceptions to a dress code or modified uniforms, and relaxed "no food or drink" and "no-sitting" policies.

CAREER DIALOGUES

Career dialogues are an important tool before and after maternity transitions, and for employee development in general. Unlike annual performance appraisals, which typically focus on the evaluation of the individual's assigned duties and tasks, while noting areas of strength or areas for improvement, **career dialogues** are future-focused and highlight opportunities as well as possibilities. They also present opportunities for the employer to gain more understanding and perspective regarding your career-related goals. To maintain the momentum of a career dialogue, it should be regarded as something ongoing. Discussions should be held frequently, such as once every quarter or as opportunity necessitates. These conversations should not be viewed as a "one and done" activity. If you have not been engaging in these types of conversations with your employer prior to your pregnancy announcement, suggest it to your employer.

"The moment I told my employer I was pregnant, no further mention was made of advancing my career within the organization, though it had been an ongoing and regular dialogue prior to that point." - Employee Quote

Career Dialogues: Strategies that Work

You may feel anxious or nervous now that you have announced your pregnancy to your employer. You may be unsure about how a maternity leave will affect your career development within the organization, and your future in general. Use the career dialogue as an opportunity to voice these concerns. Below, you will find strategies to appropriately create an open dialogue.

Proven Positive	Good to Avoid
Start having discussions once you become aware of the upcoming transition to allow time for effective planning and transition.	Do not have the conversation too late. If you have to begin your leave earlier than expected, you may not have sufficient time to put plans in place with your employer.
Practice active listening. Listen carefully to what your employer is saying, and check that you understand what is being said by reflecting back and paraphrasing in your own words.	It is sometimes common for employers to make assumptions about whether or not pregnant or adopting employees will be returning to work after a leave. If you do not feel comfortable discussing this subject with confidence, wait until you are.
In large and midsize organizations, discuss your possible career paths with your employer, and speak with colleagues in other positions within the organization. In small organizations, outline your career development and advancement opportunities with your employer and discuss ways to reach personal and professional goals in the workplace.	Do not feel that you have to follow the same path as other employees with the same job title or as other working mothers. Remember that not everyone shares the same career aspirations, and that these can change over the course of your career.
Seek out information about the options and resources that are available to you prior to the maternity leave and upon your return to work (e.g., flexible work schedules, job-sharing, mentors or maternity buddies).	If your employer does not give information to you, do not assume that options are nonexistent. Be proactive to find relevant information.
Discuss how much you would like to engage in work activities (e.g., training, team meetings) while on maternity leave and make your employer aware that plans can change after the baby comes. While on leave, some women do not think they will want to be engaged while others expect to be actively involved, yet both may change their minds once the baby arrives.	Do not feel pressured to engage in work activities while on maternity leave. Employers cannot put your job at risk if you choose not to engage in work-related activities during your leave.
Discuss the return to work plan, recognizing that it may change over time. Make a plan with your employer to revisit the plan during the maternity leave and before transitioning back to work.	Do not expect the return to work plan to be a static document. For maximum effectiveness, the return to work plan should evolve with changing employee and organizational circumstances.
Be honest about questions you are unable to answer because you cannot predict the future.	Do not make promises you cannot keep.

Proven Positive	Good to Avoid
Your employer will likely have access to more information about new projects or services so ask about these opportunities, if you are interested. It is impossible for an employer to identify your interest in something if they are unaware that you are interested.	Do not feel forced into a career goal that you do not want to buy into. In order to increase the likelihood of engagement and goal attainment, it is essential that you feel motivated to do something, and not that you *should* have to do it. Balancing multiple roles requires that you only take on the roles you feel comfortable with.

In addition to these topics, in preparation for the maternity leave, career dialogues can also include:

· A transition plan for all current projects and responsibilities.

· A transition plan for returning from leave that aligns with your career plan. If the transition plan involves other **stakeholders** (e.g., job-sharing upon return to work), these stakeholders should be contacted to discuss these arrangements prior to your leave.

PREPARING FOR THE TRANSITION

Practical considerations and actions to be implemented as a result of the career dialogue should be documented so that there is a record of what was agreed to. This will help each party achieve a smoother transition with minimal misunderstandings.

Similarly, transition discussions with your employer can also provide you with an opportunity to plan how your responsibilities will be handled while you are on leave. The option chosen—hiring a replacement, distributing the work between remaining team members, or postponing project-related work—will depend on a number of factors, including your position within the organization, the nature of the business, and the skill sets of other employees. Regardless of which option is chosen, discuss with your employer how your knowledge will be captured and transferred to another employee before the start of your leave. Ideally, the transition will allow for an overlap of time both before and after the leave with any replacements, if this option is chosen. Setting a plan for knowledge transfer helps prepare your employer for the unexpected (e.g., if you need to start your leave early, or if you choose to not return to work following your leave) to ensure appropriate steps are taken to preserve and retain valuable organizational knowledge and technical experience.

Understanding Colleague and Customer Reactions

Consider how the transition and the leave will impact internal and external colleagues and customers. When you decide to disclose your pregnancy or adoption, steps can be taken to involve stakeholders in conversations regarding the transition, if relevant (e.g., whom customers will be able to contact while you are on leave).

Take the time to identify everyone who may be impacted by the upcoming transition. Once all stakeholders are identified, you and your employer can begin to develop a communication plan about what information will be shared, including a plan for transitioning colleagues into new roles and responsibilities in your absence. Ongoing communication between you, your employer, and stakeholders and colleagues will ensure that everyone knows what to expect and has an opportunity to have input into plans.

Be prepared to encounter a range of reactions upon your announcement. Some colleagues and stakeholders will be thrilled and excited by your news, while others may be anxious or frustrated over possible transition scenarios (e.g., will your position be backfilled while you are away or will your work be split between your colleagues). Communicating about the transition and how it will be managed will mitigate any concerns that colleagues and stakeholders may have. Discuss anticipated and actual responses with your employer so that you can work collaboratively to maintain stakeholder relationships.

PRE-MATERNITY LEAVE EXIT INTERVIEW

Ask your employer to conduct a maternity leave **exit interview** so that you are given the opportunity to provide your organization with feedback on the quality of support you received and the planning processes during the pre-maternity leave period.

Suggested Talking Points:

· The aspects of your job and the organization that you enjoy the most, and the least.

· The resources you need from the organization, and your colleagues, to be successful in your position.

· How the organization can better support and communicate with new and expectant mothers.

- Suggestions to improve the pre-maternity leave transition process.

- How you believe the organization's policies and procedures regarding maternity leave are currently stated and communicated, and how you think the organization can improve.

RETURN TO WORK PLAN

Having a **return to work plan** in place before your leave starts will help facilitate your transition back to work. Although it may change while you are on maternity leave, having a basic plan in place ensures a smoother transition. Steps should also be made to adapt or modify the plan prior to your return to work.

"Having a plan to reintegrate employees back into the workforce, so that they feel valued and are seen as valuable, is essential." - Employer Quote

Suggested Talking Points:
- Date of expected return.

- Your responsibilities regarding notification of return to work (e.g., some organizational policies require the employee to provide written notice six weeks prior to returning to work).

- The return to work plan should allow for weekly or biweekly meetings between you and your employer after your return to help support your transition back into the workplace. A review should also occur within the first couple of months of your return so that you can review the career objectives established from the career dialogue prior to your leave.

- Re-onboarding and reintegration actions (e.g., support, assessment of skills, safety orientation, recertification such as first aid). Determine whether you need any additional training, information, or re-onboarding training, and request the support from your employer.

- Discuss career options (e.g., what positions may be available within the organization upon your return).

- Work schedule options (e.g., soft return or a graduated return to full-time hours, flexible hours, teleworking).

- Roles and responsibilities (e.g., who is responsible for putting the different parts of the return to work plan in place).

- Handover (i.e., identify how the handover of responsibilities will take place).

Employers play a key role in managing transitions and making the process a positive experience for new and expectant employees. Therefore, it is important for you to involve your employer so that they are given the opportunity to communicate their support, engage in career dialogues, and establish a comprehensive transition and return to work plan with you. Having these steps put in place will help you feel secure, supported, and valued going into your leave. Further, what you need to do and how the organization will assist you will be clear, alleviating any concerns about your job, your career, and your return to work.

If your employer is not working with you to make the transition a positive, transparent experience, you should consider connecting with your human resources department, provincial labour board, or the Canadian Human Rights Commission to seek advice and support.

Sample Checklist - Prior to Maternity Leave

☐ Determine if you have any specific accommodation requirements regarding your pregnancy.

☐ Find out whether your employer has any information that explains what you need to do and what support is available (e.g., maternity leave policy and procedures, flexible working policies, employee support networks, relevant external support).

☐ If applicable, ask your employer to conduct a health and safety risk assessment.

☐ Be proactive and schedule regular meetings with your manager/supervisor (or relevant others) to:

- Engage in career dialogues.

- Discuss any changes to health and safety and modifications to work accommodations.

- Discuss how the workload will be managed in your absence.

- Develop plans for a replacement/coverage if your position is being backfilled.

- Discuss when and how you will transfer your knowledge to other members of the organization.

- Discuss what kind of contact you would like to have with your employer during your leave (e.g., you may plan times to have phone calls or send e-mails to stay up-to-date on organizational changes).

☐ Create a return to work plan to:

- Establish a tentative return to work.

- Determine when your employer needs to know of your official return to work date (e.g., three weeks prior to your return to work date).

During the Maternity Leave

While on maternity leave you are still considered an employee. To avoid the risk of being "out of sight, out of mind," there are a few things you can and should do to keep yourself visible to your employer.

ENACT AND REVISE THE COMMUNICATION PLAN

If you established a communication plan with your employer prior to your leave, you can re-evaluate and/or revise the plan's details while on leave to determine the best type and frequency of communication for you. For example, if you want more or less communication, or communication on specific items, make sure to let your employer know.

Keep in mind that while Canadian legislation permits employers to engage in reasonable contact with employees during maternity leave, you are under no obligation to maintain contact with your employer.

Although small changes may not seem like a big deal, such as where files are stored or what policies state regarding everyday processes (e.g., submitting expenses, ordering supplies and resources), a number of small changes over the course of a year can be a lot of change to come back to all at once. It may seem trivial to want to know every single change that occurs while on leave but your role could be impacted by any number of adjustments in the workplace and everyone responds to change differently.

For example, you and your employer may agree to an e-mail update every two months for matters regarding administrative functions, but you may agree to updates within forty-eight hours for staffing changes, internal job postings, or training opportunities.

"The most important thing is that the individual be taken into consideration. Some women want to stay in touch, some don't; some want to extend their leave; some can't wait to come back. A good program will involve connecting with women, talking about options, and giving her choices." - Employer Quote

Sample Communication Plan

Name: _____ **Date:** _____

Preferred e-mail address: _____

Preferred contact number: _____

Change	When to Update	Communicated by Who	Preferred Method of Communication	Update Reintegration Plan	Date of Communication
Promotional and Training Opportunities	Within 48 hours	Manager or Supervisor	Phone	N/A	Jan 5, 2016
Administrative Processes (e.g., ordering supplies)	Every 2 months	Office Manager	E-mail	Yes, meet with Office Manager upon return to clarify questions	March 10, 2016

Update the Return to Work Plan

Workplace changes that occurred while you were away on maternity leave may impact your reintegration back into the workplace. For example, while you were on leave the organization may have introduced new software or may have new rules to comply with regrading occupational health and safety. If your employer followed the agreed upon communication plan, you will be in a better position to ask for reorientation and re-onboarding if necessary.

Aside from changes in the workplace, your own plans may have changed; you may want to return to work earlier than originally stated, you may want to delay your return, or you may not return at all. As an employee, it is your responsibility to communicate these changes so your employer can support your transition in the best way possible.

RETURN TO WORK LOGISTICS

Returning to paid work after maternity leave can sometimes feel chaotic, so it is important to plan ahead, get organized, and begin to establish your new routine.

In the Workplace

It will likely be your employer's responsibility to ensure that workplace logistics are in place prior to your return. However, it is still worthwhile to connect with your employer to send a friendly reminder four to six weeks prior to your planned return to work date to ensure your employer is coordinating everything you will need. If you are a contractor, you may be responsible for coordinating things yourself.

"Returning from maternity leave I was ignored. I was in a weird zone where I wasn't treated like a new employee (onboarding) and I wasn't treated as a valuable asset. I was out of the loop and not immediately useful. I felt like an afterthought that nobody cared about."
- Employee Quote

On the Home Front

Your return to employment will also be an adjustment on the home front; it may take a few weeks or even months for everyone to adjust to the new routine.

If you are using a day care or day home provider, you may want to try a few practice drop-offs and pick-ups before you actually return to work.

The following is a list of some additional ideas to consider:

· Explore options for emergency childcare. If you are using family members or neighbours as emergency backup options, ensure you provide them with important information such as your place of work, the childcare provider, food preferences, daily routines, and medical information.

· In the event of an emergency with your child be sure to communicate your preferred process to your employer. For example, if your childcare provider contacts your employer due to a child's illness, do you want to be notified during a meeting?

· Know and understand your childcare provider's policies, especially regarding illness, payment, and withdrawal.

· Know and understand your employer's policies regarding family related leave, such as in the case your child becomes sick and childcare is not an option.

· If your budget can afford it, think about keeping a small stockpile of necessities and medical supplies for when your child becomes sick (e.g., diapers, rash cream, treatments for cold, flu, fever, dehydration, first aid kit). If your child is attending childcare with other children, it is not uncommon to experience ten or more colds and flus the first year in childcare.

· Keep important numbers and addresses handy such as numbers to twenty-four hour health information, doctors' offices and walk-in clinics, and other community support services.

· Try to plan and prepare meals ahead of time and if possible, discuss how others may be able to share this responsibility.

· Think about how others in your household could support you in picking up and dropping off your child to childcare.

CONFIDENT COMPETENCE

Many women on maternity leave report a loss of confidence when returning to work. It is a phenomenon that extends not just to women who are experiencing maternity leave transitions, but to other types of leaves that result in disengaging from work for extended periods of time (e.g., medical leave, extended vacation, or sabbaticals). You may even question your confidence when returning to a role that you have successfully performed for several years. While it is unfortunate, it is also a common experience even though it is rarely supported by a corresponding decline in skills and abilities.

In the book, *The Confidence Code: The Science and Art of Self-Assurance - What Women Should Know*, authors Katty Kay and Claire Shipman explored factors associated with women's career success, and noted that confidence is equally important as competence.[53] Accessing professional development opportunities while on maternity leave can be one way to boost your confidence when reintegrating into the workplace. Professional development can also be critical in rapidly changing industries, such as technology, and research and development, in which employees are constantly learning.

Employers can offer a range of optional learning opportunities to employees on maternity leave, such as webinars, distance courses, conferences, conference calls, and subscriptions to relevant industry publications. It is important to ask your employer what may be available. You may also want to consider asking for reimbursement related to costs associated with any of the previously noted opportunities (e.g., parking, travel, childcare).

If your employer does not provide development opportunities while you are on maternity leave, you can access or create your own. What types of professional development activities you access may also be impacted by how much time you have to dedicate to these pursuits and the support and resources you need to follow through on them (e.g., childcare, money).

The following is a list of some low or no-cost ideas for developing your competence:

· **Stay connected**: Use social media such as LinkedIn, Pinterest, Instagram, Twitter, and Facebook to stay connected to and network with colleagues in your current career or in potential careers. If you have not already done so, set up a social media profile, such as LinkedIn, to stay connected to your areas of interest. You can also join special interest groups/forums through LinkedIn. Expanding your network in this way is also a great strategy to learn about different career opportunities and organizations.

· **Explore the Internet**: Look up TedTalks, which is a free platform that offers a range of inspiring and provocative talks on a host of topics. Massive Open Online Courses (MOOCs), such as those through coursera.org, are typically free or low cost no-credit modules on a range of interest areas. As the learner, it is often up to you how much or how little you decide to participate in each MOOC.

· **Peer mentorship group**: Join or start a peer group for other working mothers. You can share career successes and concerns, and obtain support and advice from peers. Your peers may have other ideas for professional development you have not considered.

- **Webinars**: Check with your professional association or other relevant organizations to determine if there are any upcoming webinars. Webinars are typically recorded and e-mailed out to participants afterwards, so you can usually access the webinar when it is most convenient for you.

- **Podcasts**: Check out Websites like mindtools.com and manager-tools.com, which offer a number of free podcasts and print resources to support skill development and acquisition for managers and individual contributors.

- **Think local**: Learn about community organizations such as public libraries, community centres, and colleges that often have free or reduced cost training, seminars, and information sessions.

- **Mentorship**: Consider finding or becoming a mentor. There are benefits to receiving mentorship and being a mentor. Mentorship conversations can occur formally or informally, such as over the phone or at a local coffee shop.

- **Volunteer**: Explore causes and organizations you feel strongly about or that may give you contacts and experience to support your interests and hobbies. If you cannot commit to a regular volunteer opportunity, consider volunteering for a onetime event or contact the organization to determine if they need any help or support that can be done from home.

"My maternity leave was an incredibly positive turning point in my career. I did a lot of reflection and career exploration. I thought of it as a professional gap year." - Employee Quote

COMEBACK COACHING

People enlist the support of a career coach for a variety of reasons. **Comeback coaching** provides career transition support to mothers returning to employment after maternity leave or an extended period of leave for raising a family.

Career and life are inseparable and impact one another in a reciprocal manner. Every working mother experiences the return to work transition uniquely and could benefit from extra support from an objective and helpful third party. Comeback coaching can begin in the weeks prior to your projected return to work date, and can continue into the first few months after your actual return, or as the particular situation determines.

It can be difficult for many individuals (not just mothers), even those with extensive career and life experience, to identify or articulate career goals, which in turn makes it difficult for your employer to provide you with the means and support necessary to develop and leverage your strengths. Comeback coaching is a strategy that can have a positive impact for both you and your employer.

Comeback coaching enables you to build confidence and gain clarity on your career goals so you can re-establish the career dialogue with your employer upon your return to work. Comeback coaching may be something you choose to seek out on your own, or you can ask your employer what support may be available through work.

COMBATTING THE IMPOSTER SYNDROME

The **imposter syndrome** is a well-researched phenomenon in social psychology that extends to both males and females. It suggests that individuals who experience the imposter syndrome are more likely to attribute their accomplishments to *external* factors (e.g., luck, fate, the actions of others) rather than to *internal* factors (e.g., intelligence, persistence, hard work, good ideas). Consequently, the individual may feel like a fraud or an imposter, and feel as though they will soon be "outed" by others and discovered for their real competence and talents, which the individual perceives to be lacking. Imposters often report lacking confidence, which may come as a surprise to colleagues and peers. It is a common experience that extends to all types of people across all types of careers.

"All of a sudden, I have a hard time understanding basic stuff in my job and I forgot a lot of information as well. I feel like I started a new job even though I came back in a job I have been doing for the past seven years." - Employee Quote

If you recognize some characteristics of yourself in the previous description, there are some steps that you can take to combat the imposter in you. In the following section, you will find some tips and strategies to challenge the imposter syndrome and boost your confidence. Improving your confidence often requires a conscious effort on your part and everyone realizes change at a different rate, so try different strategies over an extended period of time.

- **Avoid upspeak:** When making a statement, avoid using upspeak (e.g., intonation) at the end of a statement as it makes the speaker sound tentative or unsure of herself and her statement; it sounds as though you are asking a question.

  Example

  With upspeak: "My top three strengths are communication, strategic thinking, and building relationships?"

  Without upspeak: "My top three strengths are communication, strategic thinking, and building relationships."

- **Avoid minimizers:** Avoid words or phrases that dismiss you or your contributions.

  Examples

  "It's *only* me, Andrea." versus "It's me, Andrea."

  "I *just* have something to say." versus "I have something to say."

- **Practice power poses:** Social psychologist Amy Cuddy suggests that when we stand in postures that exude confidence, we convey to both ourselves and to others that we are confident. You can practice power poses before and during important situations such as job interviews, dealing with a difficult co-worker, and as part of your normal daily routine.

  For examples of the types of power poses you can try, watch Amy Cuddy's TedTalk, *Your Body Language Shapes Who You Are.*[54]

- **Explain intent before content:** Women are often rated more negatively than men by both men and women when they communicate in an assertive way. One strategy to address this is to explain your intent/provide context (why you are making the point) before the content (your point).

  Example

  Without context: "I'm not onboard with the direction of this strategy."

  With context: "I see this as a matter of fiscal and social responsibility, so I'm not onboard with the direction of this strategy."

To see more on providing context before your statement, you can watch the Behavioral Science Guys' YouTube video, *One Simple Skill to Curb Unconscious Gender Bias.*[55]

· **Take stock**: For many, our inner critic is often the harshest, but it is important to recognize that you are also well positioned to be your best advocate and supporter; after all, you are the expert on yourself. While you can quickly forget all your great accomplishments, you need to be purposeful in recognizing all that you have experienced and achieved, not just in your career, but also in health, relationships, education, finance, travel, leisure, and hobbies.

A maternity leave career transition is an opportune time to take a comprehensive inventory of your knowledge, skills, experience, training and education, career and personal accomplishments, and networks and contacts. Completing an inventory like this can boost your confidence and identify interests or career alternatives not previously considered. People typically adjust better to transition periods when they perceive options compared to when no options are identifiable. It can also help you to recognize skills and competencies, which you can promote to employers. An example is provided in the following table.

Knowledge Inventory Table	
Education and training (Programs and classes I have completed)	
Skills (Things I do well)	
Knowledge (Topics I know a lot about)	
Network (People I know in and outside of my career)	
Experience (Industries and organizations I have worked or volunteered with)	
Accomplishments (Career and personal achievements I am proud of)	
Resources (Things, organizations, and people I can draw on for help and support)	

Strengths Finder 360 Exercise

Complete a **strengths finder 360 exercise** by reaching out to supportive individuals to further understand what others see as your strengths and gifts. Identify five people, perhaps from different environments and groups (e.g., work, volunteering, friends/family, church). Ask these five people to identify your top five strengths and record their answers on the below table. Each person will provide you with a unique perspective either affirming what you already know, or pointing out qualities you may have previously overlooked as strengths. An example is provided in the following table.

Strengths Finder 360 Table						
Strengths	John (co-worker)					
1	Creative					
2	Loyal					
3	Detail oriented					
4	Dependable					
5	Strategic					

Identify and Reframe Limiting Beliefs

Many people believe in Alexander Graham Bell's famous quote, "When one door closes, another opens." Some people even adopt this metaphor to explain various career transitions. While this attitude is often viewed positively, it could also be viewed as a barrier. It is important to recognize that doors can be reopened once they are shut; after all, this is the function of a door...to be opened and closed more than once.

An important part of effectively managing your maternity leave career transition is identifying, challenging, and reframing limiting beliefs. **Limiting beliefs** are often based on assumptions versus evidence, and tend to be dichotomous, meaning an "either-or" mindset. Some keywords to listen for that may indicate a limiting belief include absolutes (i.e., always, never) and words that convey obligation or limited option (e.g., must, should, have to, need to).

Use the following table to identify your limiting beliefs and challenge yourself to reframe them positively.

Limiting Belief	Reframed Belief
Being a good mother means *never* working outside the home.	I can be a good mother if I stay at home or return to paid work.
I *should* pursue a career that is in line with my education.	My education and training is transferable and valuable in other industries and careers.

Define Success

If you are like most working mothers, when asked to define career and life success, you may come up with words like, happy, enjoy what I do, meaningful, flexibility, or financial security. Coming up with a definition of success can be challenging but with the right tools and support, it can be incredibly motivating and validating. The difficulty in creating actionable steps using the words above is that they are vague, subjective, or socially accepted indicators of success (e.g., career success is making a six-figure salary and climbing the corporate ladder). A better method for determining your definition of success is to begin with an evaluation of your own values.

When we look at societal expectations of success, we see that these definitions are often based on values (e.g., money and status). When being met, values can keep us feeling happy and/or motivated. While values are often core components of your career satisfaction, your values may change in response to specific life events. For example, having a baby and experiencing a maternity leave career transition may be a trigger for a change in values. It is important to recognize that your definition of success changes when your values do, so it is good practice to periodically reflect on your values to determine their impact on what success means to you. Further, being clear on your values will help you determine what you may need to do differently in order to achieve your ideal vision of success.

Complete the following exercise to begin building your definition of career success. Once you have selected all the values that are important to you, narrow them down and prioritize your values by limiting them to the top ten most important values, then to the top five critical values. Use the blank space to include other values not listed, if applicable.

Career Values	
Achievement	Influence
Advancement	Leadership
Adventure	Learning
Aesthetically Pleasing	Mentally Challenging
Affiliation	Meticulous
Artistic Expression	Not Physically Demanding
Autonomy	Own Pace
Belonging and Friendship	Physical Challenge
Benefits Society	Predictability and Stability
Calm	Public Service
Competence	Recognition and Appreciation
Competition	Research and Development
Cooperation	Respect
Creativity	Safety
Ethics	Security
Expertise	Status
Fast Paced	Technology
Flexibility	Travel
Fun and Humour	Variety
Helping Others	Work/Life Integration
High Salary	Work With My Hands
Independence	Working With Others
Other:	Other:
Other:	Other:
Other:	Other:

Life Values	
Acceptance	Humour
Achievement	Independence
Adventure	Intimacy
Autonomy	Justice
Balance	Leadership
Beauty	Learning and Knowledge
Caring	Loyalty
Challenge	Mindfulness
Community Service	Morality
Contribution	Open-Minded
Creativity	Practicality
Dependability	Passion
Education	Purpose
Fame	Respect for Nature
Family	Safety
Fitness	Self-Acceptance
Friendship	Self-Awareness
Fun	Self-Reliance
Generosity	Simplicity
Growth and Development	Spirituality/Religion
Hard-Working	Stability
Health	Tolerance
Helpfulness	Tradition
Humility	Travel
Other:	Other:
Other:	Other:
Other:	Other:

My top ten most important career values are:

1.	6.
2.	7.
3.	8.
4.	9.
5.	10.

My top ten most important life values are:

1.	6.
2.	7.
3.	8.
4.	9.
5.	10.

My top five critical career values are:

1.
2.
3.
4.
5.

My top five critical life values are:

1.
2.
3.
4.
5.

Based on my top five career and top five life values, my definition of success is:

_____

_____

_____

After reviewing your definition of success take a few moments to reflect on what, if anything, you may need to do differently to achieve your definition of success and make a note of your ideas below.

Action steps I can take to achieve my definition of success:

_____

_____

_____

Note that it is unlikely one role (e.g., paid employment) will satisfy all of your values so consider what other roles and activities could address your critical values, not satisfied by paid employment, and make a note of your ideas below.

_____

_____

_____

Post-Maternity Leave/Reintegration

Perhaps you have been gone for several weeks or several months, and it is almost time to return to the workplace. While on leave you may have had little to no communication with your employer; as a result, you may feel "out of the loop" with a mixture of emotions ranging from nervous and anxious to excited. You may even feel a blend of emotions on your first few days back at work. There are things that you can do to ease the transition and reintegrate back into your role, your team, and your workplace. For instance, you may begin by working part-time to ease back into your role; however, if this formal option is not available to you, consider less formal ways of re-engaging. One informal option is to go back to work mid-week so you only have to work a few days before the weekend. You can also book lunches, coffees, and meetings with colleagues, stakeholders, your manager/supervisor, etc. and let them catch you up on what has been happening within the organization. Your employer may also equip you with resources to facilitate your career development upon your return; these resources may come in the form of return to work interviews, and mentorship/sponsorship opportunities.

"When I returned from maternity leave, I felt displaced. Yes, my 'job' was secure, but many of my responsibilities were transitioned to other employees and were not returned to me. There was no re-orientation, and no one had the time to spend with me." - Employee Quote

RETURN TO WORK INTERVIEW

When you left for maternity leave, you may have participated in an exit interview with your employer. Depending on when you last discussed your return to work plan, you may want to have a **return to work interview** after you have had time to reintegrate back into your work. You may want to work for about a month before having this discussion with your employer so you have a better feel for what challenges and opportunities lie ahead. However, depending on your situation, this discussion may need to happen sooner.

This conversation is a great time to re-engage and continue the career dialogue, assess how the reintegration is going, and determine what further support and assistance you may require. Discussing actions that are needed from both you and your employer to support your personal goals is necessary to identify how your employer will support you along the way.

Suggested Talking Points:

· Express what has been the best or most satisfying aspects of returning to work.

· Express what has been the most challenging aspects of returning to work.

· Let your employer know whether you will need additional support and resources to be successful in returning to work.

· Discuss your career goals and expectations moving forward.

MENTORSHIP AND SPONSORSHIP

Although we previously noted the use of the buddy system, this strategy may be specific to a certain life occurrence (e.g., maternity leave career transition), while mentorship and sponsorship can be enacted at any point in the working mother's career, independent of maternity leave career transitions. Although both mentors and sponsors support the working mother's career development, the nature of each relationship is unique.

Mentorship is a developmental relationship where one individual with more knowledge and experience guides the lesser experienced individual. Mentors can be great confidants who offer advice, listen to your concerns, and support and coach you through problems and opportunities.[56]

Mentors are often:

· Internal or external to the working mother's place of employment.

· Aware of the working mother's career and life goals.

· Functioning in an advisory or coaching role.

· *Indirectly* responsible for the career advancement of the working mother.

Sponsorship is characterized as having support from an ally (usually a more senior employee) in the organization who has the power to effect change and actively advocate for career building opportunities. Mentoring alone, without the benefit of sponsorship, may not be enough to carry a high potential employee to the next level. In large organizations, would-be-sponsors include individuals who are two levels higher with a line of sight to your role, and in smaller firms, they are individuals who are founders or presidents.[57]

Sponsors (or advocates) are often:

· Internal to the organization or the working mother's professional community.

· Aware of the working mother's career and life goals.

· Advising on relevant career opportunities.

· *Directly* responsible for the career advancement of the working mother.

· Advocating for specific assignments or promotions on behalf of the employee.

While both mentorship and sponsorship can support the development of a working mother's career, there are several unique benefits related to sponsorship that benefit both the employee and the organization.[58] Specifically, sponsorship can:

· Identify and accelerate the careers of high performers within the organization.

· Assist working mothers to address specific challenges within their roles.

> **Tips for identifying and pursuing a mentor:**
>
> • Consider people in your network you respect such as past instructors, coworkers, or bosses.
>
> • If you belong to a professional association, contact them to see if they facilitate mentoring opportunities.
>
> • Look for mentoring candidates who have more experience than you or have achieved similar things you desire to achieve.
>
> • Consider having more than one mentor for different goals.
>
> • Explore you career goals and be ready to articulate what you hope to accomplish to potential mentors.
>
> • Explain why you would like to pursue a mentoring relationship with that individual.
>
> • Suggest a time commitment and process for the mentoring relationship.
>
> • Understand what the mentor will expect of you.

- Challenge and address lower female representation at senior levels within an organization by supporting the career development of women.

- Improve the working mother's level of reported career satisfaction and organizational commitment.

- Lead to higher-performing teams and leaders.

- Lead to increased diversity at senior levels.

Although both mentorship and sponsorship have pros and cons, you cannot benefit from either if you are not actively seeking out these opportunities! Your organization may offer official programs, or you may need to seek these opportunities out yourself. If you are seeking a mentor, you should approach individuals in or outside of your organization whom you admire. If you are seeking a sponsor, seek individuals in your organization who have the power to make things happen, and propel your career. To attract sponsors you must demonstrate your skills, strengths, and work ethic, and it must be made known to colleagues and senior leaders.[59] You will be more likely to earn a sponsorship if you build a reputation within your organization that you are consistently committed to your career development.

Tips for attracting a sponsor:

- Prepare an elevator speech about current projects you are working on and the value you are adding.

- Manage your career — take the time to evaluate your skills, growth areas, and interests. Know where you want to go in the organization. Ask for feedback and follow it.

- Aim for multiple sponsors with different points of view.

- Keep sponsors up to date with your accomplishments, and thank them for efforts taken.

- Be aware that your actions reflect on you and your sponsor.

- Start considering how you, too, can champion colleagues.

- *Catalyst* research shows that sponsors themselves advance further and faster because they're investing in talent that will lead the organization in the future.

"It's not who you know, but who knows you." - Allyson Zimmerman

Customizing Your Career
ALTERNATIVE/FLEXIBLE WORK ARRANGEMENTS

To date, Canada provides job protection status for women on maternity leave, but does not have any policy mandating flexible arrangements for working mothers.[60] With a lack of time and work-life integration being the biggest problems that new mothers face when returning to the workplace, we encourage you to be proactive and discuss your needs with your employer and, if applicable, talk about the possibility and suitability of flexible or alternative arrangements to your typical work schedule and/or environment.

Returning to work following a maternity leave can be a difficult transition, and sometimes it is no longer feasible to work according to your previous schedule. As an employee, a number of flexible work arrangements may be available to you. Below we describe some common alternative approaches that may suit both your needs and those of your employer. If you are interested in an alternative work schedule, you should discuss this option with your employer as soon as possible, and preferably before you make the transition back to work.

"Companies need to be flexible when dealing with individuals on maternity leave. A 'one size fits all' approach does not work for everyone." - Employer Quote

Starting a conversation with your manager/supervisor about flexible work options can be challenging and a source of stress and anxiety for new mothers. Many may avoid the topic because they are afraid to approach their manager/supervisor, unsure of how to ask for a more flexible work arrangement, or worried that their request will be rejected. What many new mothers do not realize is that a common reason flexible work options are not approved is because the employee never asked.

If you are considering flexible work and would like to discuss options with your employer, make sure you approach the topic with confidence. Gather the necessary information to make your case (some of which will be discussed in this section about customizing your career) and strongly position your request. Set up a meeting with your manager/supervisor and arrive prepared with a plan or written proposal in place for how you will make this arrangement work. Demonstrating that you have already put a considerable amount of thought into this plan will show how committed you are to making it work and will also increase buy-in on the part of your employer. Take the time to rehearse the conversation so that you can anticipate concerns that may be expressed by your manager/supervisor and have responses ready.

When developing a plan for alternative work arrangements, ensure that you take the time to consider not only your needs, but also the needs of your employer. While you may be requesting flexible arrangements because of reasons related to your personal life, focus the conversation on the topic of work and appeal to the bottom-line concerns of your employer. In the same way that your request for flexible work is likely motivated by personal desires or needs, present your case in an objective and business-like manner to boost the likelihood that your request will be approved.

Ask yourself and be prepared to answer questions such as: What is in it for my manager/supervisor? How will the organization benefit? Think of approaching the conversation the same way you would if asking for a raise. While requesting a pay increase may be motivated by a desire or need for greater financial support, you approach the conversation by appealing to your high level of work performance and productivity.

In the case that your employer is hesitant to fully embrace your transition to a more flexible work arrangement, propose a pilot or trial period. This will give both of you the opportunity to gather more information, identify unanticipated challenges, and work together to find ways to enhance the productivity and feasibility of the arrangement.

TELEWORK AND WORKSHIFT

Telework and **WORKshift** involve working away from the traditional office space so that you are able to work when, where, and how you are most effective and efficient. Telework is one aspect of WORKshift, but not the only form of flexible work covered by this concept. Working when and where one is most effective, whether it is from home or other locations, and flexing one's hours are both part of this alternative way of working.

Being a new mother may make it more difficult to find and maintain a balanced lifestyle when re-integrating into the workplace. The ability to work from alternative locations is an attractive option for a number of reasons. Working when and where it is most convenient for you means that you can make yourself more available for other priorities in your life. Working away from the traditional office has also been associated with a number of work-related benefits, including increased levels of productivity, motivation, and satisfaction. Because WORKshifting employees tend to be removed from many of the distracting and stressful aspects of the workplace, such as office politics and interruptions, they are often more efficient and derive greater pleasure from their work. WORKshift arrangements also lead to a number of savings for the employee, including reduced financial costs (e.g., money spent on commuting, parking, and paying for lunches), as well as temporal costs (e.g., time spent in traffic).

WORKshift or flexible work arrangements can be a win-win situation for both you and your employer when implemented correctly. However, these arrangements are not a "one size fits all," as personality and work style differences need to be considered. Before making a decision about whether telework will be a good fit for you, here are some things to consider:

Considerations Before Deciding to Telework

Do you prefer to work alone or with other people?

If you thrive on interactions with co-workers or find that being around others is a source of energy, teleworking will likely present challenges for you (unless done only part of the time, thereby complemented with days in the office). Some find that the traditional workplace gives them the motivation necessary to work, and are unable to find that same drive in less formal settings, such as a coffee shop or home office.

Would you consider yourself to be self-motivated?

A big part of deciding if teleworking is right for you involves taking the time to honestly evaluate your work style. While self-motivation is one important factor, teleworking is ideally suited for those individuals who are also skilled in planning and organizing, and are relatively independent, effective time managers, disciplined, not easily distracted, and technically proficient.

Can your work be done from a remote location?

Pragmatically, you must consider whether or not the type of work that you do is well suited to working from a distance. Just like not all people are a good fit for telework, not all jobs are appropriate for this type of arrangement. Think about what your typical day at the office looks like and ask yourself whether you can complete these same tasks from another location. When making this decision, be sure to also consider the needs of your employer, customers, clients, and other stakeholders.

Do you have a functional alternative space where you can work?

Whether it is at home, in a coffee shop, or at another location, make sure you have a space that you can be both comfortable and focused on your work. It is also important to remember that teleworking is not a viable childcare solution and some employers may require proof of childcare for teleworking parents. Mixing work with children can be appealing, but it typically leads to diminished results in both areas.

Tips for Teleworking Mothers

- **Minimize distractions**: Your office or workspace should be free from distractions. This means staying away from things like the television, household chores, and other family responsibilities while working from home, except during scheduled breaks. Let other people in your household know when you are working and that you are not to be interrupted during this time. Part of minimizing distractions also includes keeping your workspace organized, just like you would in the office.

- **Take breaks**: When you are not working at the office and adhering to a strict schedule, in can be easy to forget that you need to step away from your work periodically during your day. Practice good habits such as taking occasional breaks and giving yourself a lunch hour if you plan to work through the day. Giving your brain and your body a break is not only healthy, but it also allows you to re-charge and return to your work not only refreshed, but also more productive.

- **Maintain your focus**: When working from home it can be tempting to prioritize your house or family responsibilities, and to let work slip through the cracks. Some people find that they can sit at home with their work open all day and not make any progress because there are so many other things going on around them. Beginning each day with a clear plan, which may include outlining specific outcomes or deliverables, will help you stay on track.

- **Practice good "distance dialogue"**: Communication is a vital component of teleworking success. Clear, timely, and frequent communication is an important responsibility on your part and for your employer. Discuss in advance what style of communication is preferred (e.g., e-mail, phone or conference calls, in-person meetings) and be sure to negotiate when and how much communication will be maintained. Keeping in touch with your co-workers and other colleagues is also important for maintaining relationships, building trust, and strengthening team performance.

- **Track your time:** Whether you are a salaried or contracted employee, tracking your time working offsite can help you, as well as your employer, clearly determine if enough work is being accomplished in the time being paid for and if you are being compensated adequately for your work.

"Organizations can help with providing the opportunity to telework so that [new mothers] don't have to lose touch either during maternity leave or if they need to take a day off to tend to a sick child." - Employee Quote

Job-sharing is an alternative work schedule where two employees voluntarily share the responsibilities, time commitment, salary, and leave of one or more positions or sets of duties.

According to a recent UK study, 90% of new mothers cited the option to job-share as being a potential factor in whether they would stay at an organization.[61] In many ways, two heads are better than one, and this is also true of job-sharing. Having the ability to share the work you do with another person not only gives you more time outside of the office, but it is also likely to improve your performance.

Having more than one person complete the tasks associated with a single position could mean double the talent.[62] When there are two sets of perspectives brought to one position, a wider range of talent and experience can be drawn upon. Having two people responsible for the same job also creates a built-in check system, with each of you being accountable to the other, thereby maintaining quality control and preventing errors on the job. Job-sharing may also mean continuous job coverage during vacations, sick leave, and other absences. This alternative also allows more freedom and flexibility to work around your personal and family life.

Considerations Before Deciding to Job-Share

Who will you job-share with?

Often times it is up to the employee to find someone who is willing to "share" your job. Not only will this person need to be someone that you are comfortable working with, but he or she must also be someone that your employer is comfortable hiring or splitting your position with if they are already an employee. Whether this person is internal or external to your workplace, you will have to ask yourself if it will be a good fit. This includes considering whether his or her personality, communication style, and skill-set will pair well with yours. This does not necessarily mean that the two of you should have *similar* skills or work styles, but rather that your experiences and perspectives are complementary to each other.[63] You should also work well with this individual on a personal level, as job-sharing will require a great deal of correspondence and coordination.

How will the duties and responsibilities associated with the job be divided?

While this decision may be left up to management, have a discussion with your job-sharing colleague about how you would like to share the responsibilities associated with your position. Would you prefer that it be divided based on tasks, workload, or days of the week? Are there any responsibilities that you would like to share? Take into consideration each of your preferences and unique skills or talents. Remember that decisions such as these are not set in stone, and that you are encouraged to have an open and ongoing discussion with your manager/supervisor, as well as your job-sharing colleague, about how things are going and if any changes or adjustments are needed.

How will the work schedule be divided?

Consider how you would like to share your work schedules and whether or not the two of you will split your time based on the day (e.g., morning and afternoon) or the week (e.g., Monday to Wednesday and Wednesday to Friday). There are many ways that you can share time spent at the office, but know that your job-sharing colleague may also have personal commitments that restrict his or her availability. Make sure that the schedule suits the needs of all parties, including your employer. Also take into consideration the amount of overlap time that may be necessary for the two of you to have each day or week to ensure that the details of your work can be discussed.

Is the position in question suited to the restructuring necessary for job-sharing?

Some roles are easier to share than others. Positions well suited to job-sharing are often those in which there is a clear division of responsibilities or tasks and the job-sharing employees communicate and achieve consensus on the roles and responsibilities of each person. Before thinking about the possibility of pursuing or requesting a job-sharing opportunity, make sure that it is feasible to divide the work between two people.

Tips for Job-Sharing Mothers

· **Learn from your co-worker:** Returning to work following maternity leave can be a challenging transition. Employers often try to pair job-sharers based on the employer's needs. You may find yourself job-sharing with someone who is also either phasing into or out of the organization. If you are job-sharing with someone more experienced who is scaling back before retirement, take this as an opportunity to learn from his or her expertise.

- **Work as a team:** Even though you are job-sharing with someone, it can be easy to fall into a pattern of working as individuals. Try and take the time to show interest in the work your colleague is doing and acknowledge his or her successes in achieving work goals, as well as your joint successes. Creating a common sense of purpose and sharing in each other's accomplishments will foster your personal and professional connection, allowing you to be more efficient in your work and effective as a team when making decisions that impact your job(s).

- **Treat each other (and be treated) as equals:** Part of working as a team also includes working as equals. Avoid competing with your job-sharing colleague and establish ground rules from the beginning to reduce competition. This could mean that you split travel equally, work the same number of days each week, and each have equal compensation and benefits. It has also been suggested that job-sharing colleagues have two performance reviews, one for your team, as well as one individually.[64]

- **Open communication:** Maintaining communication with your employer and your job-sharing colleague is essential. Having some overlap in your work shifts will encourage this, but you will also need to establish other means of connecting throughout the week. Discuss whether e-mail, shared calendars, or phone calls are most appropriate. It is also important to establish a way of communicating what tasks, assignments, or activities have or have not been finished, especially if you are sharing daily responsibilities. Finally, make sure that communication with co-workers is delivered on behalf of the "job-sharing team." You ideally want everyone to feel that communicating with one of you is the same as communicating with both of you so that your co-workers do not feel the need to repeat things to each of you.

FLEXIBLE HOURS

Flexible hours involve a schedule where employees work a full day but can vary their hours, allowing flexibility in the start and end of their workday.

- **Core time**: Hours of the day that employees are required to be at the office or otherwise accessible (e.g., 10:00 a.m. to 3:00 p.m.).

- **Flex time**: Hours of the day that employees have flexibility in when they can work.

As a new mother, working flexible hours is one way for you to address the challenges of managing the multiple responsibilities that you now have as both an employee and a parent. Varying the hours that you start and/or end your workday can give you the necessary flexibility to accommodate family and/or personal commitments, such as doctor's appointments, being home for deliveries and repair services, and picking up your child from day care. Working flexible hours may also enable you to avoid heavy rush hour traffic by commuting at less busy times of the day.

In a recent study out of Boston College, employees who had more flexible work arrangements reported a number of personal benefits, including better sleep, more exercise, and a healthier lifestyle, all of which are areas of life that are likely to diminish after becoming a parent.[65] As a result, mothers who have the opportunity to work according to a flexible schedule also tend to report less work-to-family strain. This not only benefits their personal lives, but also their ability to be more fully present and invested in their work when at the office, leading to greater overall job satisfaction.

PART-TIME WORK

It is worth noting that there is no statutory definition of what constitutes a part-time employee, as it can vary from employer to employer. However, according to Statistics Canada, an employee is considered to work part-time when they work less than thirty hours per week.[66]

During your pregnancy or maternity leave, you may have asked yourself whether you were going to take on the role of a stay-at-home mom or continue to pursue employment. Often in spite of a desire to do both, many expectant and new mothers find themselves thinking about work and family as mutually exclusive, where doing one means that you cannot do the other. This notion is supported by research, which shows that the number one reason mothers in Canada do not return to work after being away on maternity leave is a lack of access to part-time positions in their workplace.[67]

New Concept Part-Time Employment

Some working mothers can be hesitant to take up part-time employment because of the reduced compensation, marginalization on the job, and reduced career advancement opportunities that tend to be associated with these positions. To avoid this stigmatization, consider discussing **new-concept part-time employment** options with your employer. These positions often come with enhanced prestige, job satisfaction, higher income, and career opportunities for women.

In contrast to other part-time positions, these are high-status, career-oriented options that offer reduced hours to employees, often allowing working mothers to maintain prorated professional salaries and benefits. These employment opportunities encourage new mothers to continue making professional career contributions while fulfilling family responsibilities, and simultaneously allow employers to retain the talent and skill that they bring to the workplace. For more information on new-concept part-time employment, see *Beyond the Mommy Track: The Influence of a Reduced-Hours Work Schedule Program on the Work/Life Balance of Professional Women*, by Hill and Kadi, or *New-Concept Part-Time Employment as a Work-Family Adaptive Strategy for Women*, by Hill, Martinson, and Ferris.[68]

Considerations Before Deciding to Work Flexible Hours or Part-Time

How many hours a week are you available to work?

The hourly requirements for flexible and part-time positions will depend on your needs as well as those of your employer. While all part-time employees work less than thirty hours per week, the exact number of hours can vary tremendously. Prior to having a discussion with your manager/supervisor about options, consider how many hours of work you would be comfortable working per week, and whether this will be a viable option to your employer.

Can you be available during core hours/days?

Organizations often have core hours of the day or times of the year (blackout periods) when they are busiest and all employees are expected to be available. During these times flexibility may be limited. Have a discussion with your employer in advance about any foreseeable boundaries or restrictions to a flexible or part-time work schedule. The length and time of your lunch period and other breaks should also be negotiated, especially if you will be working reduced hours.

What time will you start and finish work? Will this schedule be consistent on a daily or weekly basis?

While flexible and part-time arrangements give you the opportunity to vary your working hours, it is usually best to maintain consistency in your schedule by establishing set times during which you will be available. Not only is this courteous, but clearly communicating a consistent schedule will also minimize errors. For example, if you leave the office at 3:00 p.m. every day, your co-workers will know that anything with a deadline will need to be given to you mid-afternoon, rather than at the end of the day.

How will you be contacted in the case of an emergency?

Discuss with your manager/supervisor whether it is necessary for you to be available to answer calls during a workplace emergency while out of the office. Determine an appropriate means of communication (e.g., phone) and set clear guidelines regarding under what circumstances it is appropriate to reach you outside of your work hours.

Tips for Mothers Who Work Flexible Hours or Part-Time

Maximize face time: When working a flexible schedule, you may not get the chance to see or touch base with others in the office during a typical workday. This can make it difficult to have conversations with your manager/supervisor. As a result, you may feel distanced from the organization and other staff. If you notice that you are losing touch, take the initiative to schedule time with your manager/supervisor when you are both in the office to discuss work and other topics.

Keep your flexibility consistent: While maintaining consistency may appear to be counter-intuitive to having flexibility, it is important to not confuse a flexible schedule with a casual schedule. Clearly outline with your manager/ supervisor what times you will be in the office and ensure that this is communicated to your clients, co-workers, and anyone else who may be impacted by a change in your schedule (e.g., administration and human resources). If possible, use an online scheduler that can be shared between your team members to indicate when you are available.

Maintain the quality of your work: Just because you are not working as often, does not mean you will not be working as hard. In fact, when mothers have more time to commit to their families, they tend to be more committed to producing quality work when they are on the clock. Make sure your clients, co-workers, and manager/supervisor know that they will not be getting any less from you just because of your flexible or part-time status.

Be mutually flexible: Reduced hours work best when both you and your employer are committed to this arrangement. If there are cases when you are needed at the office outside the bounds of your reduced schedule (e.g., for a meeting), flexibility must be given and received from both sides.

Stay involved: When you work flexible hours or part-time it can be easy to miss out on work events and other job related opportunities, making it more difficult to stay up-to-date on trends and professional development. Whether it is a training seminar or simply an outing with colleagues, try and stay connected with work beyond the confines of your office and regular hours.

"There needs to be a different conceptualization of what engagement looks like. It cannot just be time spent on the clock." - Employer Quote

Benefits of flexible work options to both you and your employer include:

- **Increased satisfaction**: Employees who have the ability and freedom to work according to a flexible schedule often report more satisfaction from their jobs and feeling more supported in the work environment, not only on an occupational level but also on a personal level.

- **Increased productivity**: Workplace flexibility is associated with improved morale, loyalty, and engagement, which leads to increased performance and levels of productivity. When employees are afforded the opportunity to work where and/or when it best suits their personal working style, they are likely to produce higher quality work. According to WORKshift Canada, employees who **telework** one or more days per week experience increased productivity by up to 40%.[69]

- **Lowered environmental impact**: Some flexible work arrangements allow employees to work from home, meaning that less time is spent commuting to and from work. According to the Canadian Telework Association, if one million teleworkers were to work from home one day each week, fifty million hours of time would be saved.[70] Other benefits include significant reductions in carbon dioxide emissions, fuel costs, and mileage.

- **Reduced stress**: New mothers who have the opportunity to integrate their work and home lives experience less strain, reducing overall stress and fatigue. Employees who have better work-life integration demonstrate greater overall mental and physical health.

Additional Topics to Discuss with Your Employer Before Making Alternative Work Arrangements

- How long will the modified work arrangement be in place?

- How and when will the modified work arrangement be reviewed with your employer?

- How may the modified work arrangement impact your benefits and qualifications for government programs (e.g., will you still be eligible for health benefits or pension plans)?

- What accommodations will be made if meetings, training sessions, or other important events do not fit with your alternative schedule?

- How will you be contacted if/when you are not in the office (e.g., cellphone, e-mail)?

- What impact, if any, will the modified work arrangement have on your future career development and progression with the organization?

We encourage you to take the time to think about whether alternative work arrangements are right for you and a feasible option for your workplace. It can also be of value to think of these options as temporary or a gradual return to work schedule. At the end of the day, make sure that whichever arrangement you choose is a good fit for both you and your employer, and is developed collaboratively between both of you.

MOMPRENEURS

You may have heard the term "mompreneur," but what does it really mean? According to themompreneur.com, a **mompreneur** is any mother who understands what it means to run a business and a family without sacrificing one for the other, and is actively doing so. Although the concept of mompreneur is relatively new, the representation of women and mothers in self-employment has seen substantial growth in recent years, with Industry Canada reporting a 200% increase in the number of women-owned businesses over the past two decades.[71] In fact, according to Leblanc, over 30% of small business enterprises in Canada are created and owned either solely by women or in equal partnership with men.[72]

For many years, motherhood was thought to be a lifestyle choice that interfered with work productivity and focus, especially when faced with the demands of starting one's own company. While many people assume that working mothers are less productive at work, research has shown the opposite...that having children actually trains mothers to be more efficient and effective with their time.[73] According to Tamara Monosoff, author of *The Mom Inventors Handbook*, women with children tend to already have developed critical skills that entrepreneurs need, such as patience, stamina, and persistence, making them ideal candidates for this type of work.[74]

"Many people assume that mothers returning from maternity leave get less work done. Nothing is farther from the truth. If anything, I was re-energized. I let fewer people sidetrack my day and work activities because I had to leave on time to pick up [my] kids. I feel I am more organized now with my workday than I was before kids." - Employee Quote

Mompreneurs® is Canada's fastest growing media company and networking group for women in business. After leaving a teaching career to be with her kids, Maria Locker, founder and CEO of the Mompreneurs, realized that being self-employed was the best fit not only for her, but also for her family. "Being able to work outside of the normal 9:00 to 5:00 realm is key. I love that I can opt to go on a field trip with my kids without 'checking with my boss' – I just aim to make sure everything is organized the day before so that I can put my 'out of office' reply on without being stressed about it!"

Push and Pull Factors

Making the decision to pursue self-employment is one that will take time and warrants much consideration. There are a multitude of factors that can influence this decision and either pull working mothers towards entrepreneurship and/or push them away from typical employment positions.

Below you will find a list of common push and pull factors identified by Patterson and Mavin.[75] If you are considering becoming a mompreneur, feel free to add some additional push and pull factors to the chart that you feel may be personally relevant to your own decision making process.

Push Factors	Pull Factors
Factors that push working mothers away from traditional employment, encouraging them to pursue entrepreneurship.	*Factors that pull working mothers towards, or attract them to pursue, entrepreneurship*
Inflexible employment	Appeal of independence and autonomy
Lack of promotion possibilities	The belief that business ownership might enable better work-life integration
Difficulty finding or affording day care	Increased control over scheduling and time
Time away from family	Pursuing something that you are passionate about and/or believe is of value

Considerations Before Deciding To Be a Mompreneur

Becoming a mother has a significant impact on not only your personal and family life, but also your career and professional life, bringing with it a number of questions about how you will negotiate and integrate your roles going forward as both a mother and as a working parent. Will my workplace offer enough flexibility for me to care for my child? Will I be able to find the time to attend sporting events or fieldtrips? Can I say no to overtime without it affecting my position with the organization? The experience of having and raising children can drive women to choose self-employment or entrepreneurship for many reasons, but often because of family responsibilities or through the recognition of a business opportunity thanks to the experience of motherhood.[76]

At first glance, mompreneurship seems as though it could be the answer to all of your problems, as it allows you to own your own business, contribute to the family income, and spend time with your children. However, there are a number of potential risks that come with pursuing entrepreneurship. While not all mothers who pursue entrepreneurship will experience these challenges, they are important to consider and prepare for:

- **Long, atypical hours**: While having the flexibility to set and work your own hours is appealing, most mompreneurs say they end up working even harder and more often than they did when they were employees in an organization. Although many mothers pursue mompreneurship in an attempt to better manage their time and responsibilities, research has found that entrepreneurs typically work more, rather than fewer, hours.[77] As a mompreneur, not only could you be working longer hours, you may also be working atypical hours. Whether it is after your kids go to bed, during nap time, or early in the morning, becoming a mompreneur requires the discipline to work and focus at what can often be atypical hours of the day and night!

- **Big investment**: Making the decision to become an entrepreneur will require not only a great deal of your time, but also your energy and finances. During a time in your life when most of these resources are being devoted to your family, it may seem unrealistic to simultaneously start a new business. While that does not mean it is impossible, new mothers are encouraged to consider whether they have the necessary resources to back a new company, with particular consideration given to the monetary investment. Starting up a new business can be costly, and you may find yourself in a situation where it takes longer than expected to see a return on your investment, if at all.

- **More responsibilities**: When you are working for an employer, there are a handful of responsibilities and tasks associated with the job you perform, most of which may be manageable and feasible to complete on a daily basis or by given deadlines. However, when you run your own business your responsibilities increase dramatically. One mistake commonly made by new entrepreneurs is that they have an idea for a business, but not an idea of how to run a business. If you are considering this route, make sure that you have a working knowledge about all facets of your new start-up and are prepared to manage or oversee them yourself, at least in the early stages. This includes finances, sales, marketing, inventory, tax payments, payroll, and the hiring process, to name a few. Having other skills such as organization, planning, and leadership are also important. In her book, *The Entrepreneurial Mom's Guide to Running Your Own Business*, Canadian author and co-founder of Mompreneurs®, Kathryn Bechthold offers useful steps and advice for putting ideas into action, from market research to product launch.[78]

> **Mompreneur Success Story:**
>
> As an elementary school teacher in Burnaby British Columbia and mother of three young children, Elaine Tan Comeau was no stranger to the struggle of trying to get kids organized and into their morning or evening routines. To make life easier in both the classroom and at home, Elaine designed Easy Daysies, an innovative visual daily routine chart that allows children to organize their day based on tasks or chores, allowing them to become more independent and successful. Elaine's product has been featured on the hit TV show Dragon's Den, and is now sold across Canada and the United States.

- **Increased stress**: Given the above-mentioned challenges, it likely comes as no surprise that mothers who pursue entrepreneurship often report greater levels of stress. When running your own business, especially if that business is managed from home, mothers tend to feel conflicted about how they spend their time. Ironically, while the goal of self-employment is commonly to *increase* work-life integration, mompreneurs can sometimes feel that their roles as a mother and as a businesswoman are at odds with each other, which can lead to a *decrease* in work-life integration, and ultimately have a negative impact on one's wellbeing.

Tips for Mompreneurs

- **Do something you are passionate about**: Passion is an important success factor for all employees, but especially entrepreneurs. Many mompreneurs say that their decision to become self-employed was inspired by an idea they had for an innovative new product based on their own experiences of being a mother and a desire to better the lives of their children. Doing something that you enjoy will not only prove to be more rewarding, but it can also be a great source of drive and motivation.

- **Make use of technology**: Using technology can make it easier to work when and where it is most convenient for you, whether conducting a meeting in your home office, or sending an e-mail before running an errand. Running a business remotely from any mobile device and location allows you to be mentally present at work, even when you are not at the office.

- **Separate work and home life**: This is often one of the most difficult things for mompreneurs as they often find themselves in the role of mother and businesswoman at the same time. However, when it is possible and makes sense to do so, try and separate the two so that you are able to be more efficient and focused as both a parent and as a professional. Creating official office hours for uninterrupted work or scheduling family time allows you to be fully present.

- **Be productive and purposeful with your time**: A big part of being productive with your time is eliminating interruptions. When you are working, choose an area of the house that is removed from the action and make sure that everyone in the family knows to give you some privacy. When you are with your family, make sure all electronic devices are kept on silent and if possible, kept separate. Establishing a routine and being consistent with your work schedule will also allow you to accomplish more on a daily basis.

For a more in-depth and hands-on look at mompreneurship, from the challenges of juggling a business and a family, to advice on starting and running a successful business venture, check out Amy Ballon and Danielle Botterell's book, *Mom Inc.: Raising Your Family and Your Business Without Losing Your Mind or Your Shirt*. Learn about their personal experiences as successful Canadian mompreneurs and that of other self-employed mothers across North America.[79]

Dr. Roberta Neault and Dr. Deirdre Pickerell have also recently published a resource in partnership with CERIC entitled, *Look Before You Leap: Self-Employment Survival Strategies*; this comprehensive guide to the career development of self-employed individuals is available online free of charge and can be downloaded at www.ceric.ca/publications.[80] Through the application of this resource, readers learn to evaluate their readiness for self-employment and develop strategies for building their business, including creating a business plan, marketing to clients, and managing money.

- **Schedule face time**: Being a new mother can be isolating and being self-employed can contribute to this feeling of seclusion. Make sure that you make an effort to schedule in-person meetings with clients and stakeholders over a lunch hour or in a public place that is child-friendly if you do not have access to childcare. This not only facilitates you being present in the moment, but also works to build stronger relationships with those in your network. Spending time with like-minded individuals can offer a refreshing change of pace and is a good opportunity to network and market your business.

Considerations for Diverse Populations

The traditional family is no longer the norm in Canada. There is considerable demographic variety across expectant and new mothers, and not every woman is on the same playing field when her child arrives. Challenges extend beyond financial considerations and some groups will undoubtedly have to face unique circumstances both before and after giving birth or adopting. Among mothers who are considered to be **marginalized** or disadvantaged, a disproportionate number cluster into six groups: young mothers (age twenty-five and under), first-time mothers over age forty, adoptive parents, aboriginal women, recently immigrated women, and same-sex parents. Although not all mothers in these groups would be considered marginalized, it is important to address some considerations specific to these groups. Marginalized mothers are least likely to fully capitalize on their benefits for a host of reasons. The following section outlines some common barriers that need to be overcome by these groups, and provide recommendations on how, as a marginalized mother, you can approach your career with a new found sense of empowerment.

In addition to age, other diverse populations such as adoptive parents, recent immigrants, visible minority women, aboriginal mothers, and same-sex parents each deserve consideration. Some members of these populations are less likely to be able to access paid birth benefits, while others face social, rather than financial pressures, and must cope with discrimination and social stigmatization. Indeed, some groups will face the dual challenge of financial depletion along with high levels of discrimination.

Consideration 1

Young mothers are often faced with the dual challenge of acclimating to maternal duties while continuing to develop.[81] Having a clear role identity, solid forms of social support, and guidance to adapt to the demands of parenting all contribute to successfully fulfilling your role as a new mother.[82] One of the clear links with being able to effectively parent throughout your child's life is to be educated. There is research to suggest that education positively influences self-perception of parenting abilities.[83]

Indeed, as a young woman you may have considerable aspirations and goals that you hope to achieve in your adulthood. School may be a means to achieve these goals, and it may be possible that during your pregnancy you will also be a student. However, pursuing school while adapting to the role of mother may seem daunting and overwhelming.

Consideration 2

Further, your rights as a pregnant woman pursuing education are issues that rarely get discussed. You should not feel as though you are being held back for being a mother. As a young mother, you should not be pushed out, stressed out, or punished for wanting to pursue an education while parenting. Within learning institutions there are resources that you can turn to, like your school counsellor, and a human resources department. Although legislation seems to differ across institutions and provinces, these professionals can act as a starting point to guide you through your options so you can pursue an education while experiencing the joys of first-time motherhood.

"I was a graduate student when I took my second maternity leave. I didn't take leave after the first pregnancy because we couldn't afford to lose my scholarship funding. There was very little support and no mentor who had been there to offer support or advice."
- Employee Quote

Consideration 1

The trend of becoming a parent in the later years of your life is an ongoing and ever pervasive one. The percentage of first births for women age thirty-five years or older has increased dramatically. In 2005, the rate of first-time mothers over the age of thirty-five nearly tripled at 11% compared to a mere 4% in 1987.[84] Similarly, in the United States of America this number increased eightfold, from 1% to 8%.[85] The proportion of women completing higher education has also increased quite substantially, which can provide insight into why some women are choosing to become a parent later in life. Women with an advanced maternal age are more likely to have completed schooling and have a greater accumulation of work experience than their younger counterparts. Generally, this results in an increase in financial stability, and as such, women who have children at a later age may be willing to take longer maternity leaves. If you do not get paid for your maternity leave, the option of taking a longer maternity leave may not be feasible for younger women who may experience less than favourable financial situations. However, women in this demographic may also take shorter maternity leaves (i.e., less than a year) due to loss of salary, the demanding nature of their career, or perceived negative impact to their career by taking a leave of absence.

As an experienced woman, you are often an invaluable asset to the organization. Know your worth, know that you are not easily replaceable, and know that you do not need to approach maternity leave and re-integration with an all or nothing mentality.

Consideration 2

Another consideration is that you may be juggling additional responsibilities – not only becoming a mother, but also helping your aging parents. This is called the **sandwich generation**—individuals caught between the often conflicting demands of caring for children and for parents. Women often shoulder much of the child-care responsibility within two-parent households, even when both parents are in the labour force.[86] This also holds true for elder care, both in terms of the likelihood of providing care and in performing the most intensive tasks such as bathing, dressing, and cooking.[87] Working out a flexible work arrangement is a possibility, enabling you to be a better caregiver and a better employee.[88] As up to 35% of the sandwich generation has reportedly changed their work schedules to accommodate for these changes, it is an alternative that employers should be open to explore with you, especially when a newborn is involved.[89]

ADOPTIVE PARENTS

Consideration 1

As an adoptive parent you need to make your employer aware that your needs run parallel to any expecting mother even though you may be adopting a newborn or a slightly older child. It is often the reality that organizations experience difficulties grasping the idea that you will require the same level of support as a biological parent. As an adoptive parent you are also faced with the challenge of requiring the all-important time to bond with your child. Currently in Canada, adoptive parents are not given the fifteen weeks of employment insurance that biological mothers receive for the physical hardships of bearing a child. However, you are entitled to up to thirty-five weeks of parental benefits through employment insurance and your employer is mandated to take you back once this leave is complete.[90]

Consideration 2

Adoptive parents also deal with timelines that can be wildly unpredictable. You may be unsure about how long the adoption process will take and whether you will be successful in the adoption process. Remain open and honest with your employer; maintaining an open line of communication will ensure that no one is met with unwanted surprises. For instance, make sure your employer is aware of whether you need to travel to meet your newborn and, if applicable, how far along the biological mother is as soon as you learn the information.

"The goal of leave is the well-being of my child, and an adoptive child is at least as vulnerable and needy in terms of emotional support as a birth child." - Employee Quote

NEW IMMIGRANT MOTHERS

A survey of immigrant mothers identified social support as a key factor in accessing maternal services in Canada; however, they are also the women who reported receiving less social support during their pregnancy compared to Canadian-born mothers.[91] This can lead to feelings of isolation and seclusion.[92] The social support systems of new immigrant families are often thousands of miles away and are not always accessible.

In a study by Reitmanova and Gustafson, women often expressed a desire to spend time with someone from their community with previous maternity experience.[93] Indeed, if you are feeling isolated and lonely, there are community services offered specifically for minority women. Seek out women and groups in your area that can offer support in the form of mentorship programs. These individuals may be able to provide you with information about resources (e.g., household help, reassurance, and financial assistance), which you may not be aware of.[94]

ABORIGINAL MOTHERS

Consideration

As an aboriginal mother, you may seek mentorship to guide you along the cultural traditions your ancestors upheld during their pregnancies. That is, some aboriginal women may hold different pregnancy traditions and routines. If you have special considerations, please familiarize your employer with these traditions and rituals, so special accommodations can be made for events.[95] Being able to practice traditional rituals in an environment without stigma and judgment is imperative, and if this is something you value, make sure to let your employer know.

SAME-SEX MOTHERS

Consideration

Sometimes, it is not comfortable, nor is it necessary to share one's sexual identity within your workplace, especially if there could be negative repercussions associated with the sharing of such information. Arranging for parental leave may lead to coming out in a workplace where you may have preferred not to do so. Not surprising, some fears are that:

· Sexual identity will result in social stigmatization from employers and colleagues.

· Having a child with a same-sex partner may be met with little support and understanding.[96]

Although you may be faced with unnecessary discrimination, know that children who are raised with gay or lesbian parents do not differ from other children in terms of emotional functioning, sexual orientation, stigmatization, gender role behaviour, behavioural adjustment, gender identity, learning, and grade point averages.[97] Use these pieces of information as a tool to equip yourself if someone is unduly harsh. Similar to other diverse populations, seek the social support that is necessary to overcome hardships, and connect with others in your community (even proximally, in your organization).

Also, know your rights! In a female same-sex relationship, the partner who carries the child will receive the fifteen weeks that are allotted to women to recover from the physical hardship of birth. In addition to this time, same-sex parents are given the same amount of time as heterosexual couples for parental leave. However, for some same-sex partnerships, in vitro fertilization (IVF) or adoption may be the only viable options when considering parenthood. In most provinces and territories, same-sex partners can adopt a child together, just as opposite sex couples can. Like other adoptive or IVF parents, same-sex parents may have to attend multiple meetings or appointments, or may need to travel to meet their child, if they are using a surrogate or adopting overseas. This may require flexible work schedules and may mean unpredictable timelines. Employers will have to be ready for you to leave at a moment's notice, but by preparing them for this possibility ahead of time, you will increase the likelihood of support from your employer and decrease any potential for miscommunication.

In this section, we have outlined some important considerations relevant to unique and diverse groups of women. This section was not meant to be exhaustive, and you should be mindful that there are additional groups who may be discriminated against. One of the most important things that employees can do to mitigate the effects of being a marginalized group is to create a socially supportive work climate that enables all individuals to gather the necessary resources and tools they need to make the most of their leave. Again, it may be up to you, as an employee, to actively seek out these resources and help guide your employer in understanding how they can help you. Although it is not always an easy road, make sure that you take the time to seek social support from women who are similar to you!

Five Working Mother Mantras

Following you will find five mantras to help you stay motived in your career development and as a mother. Not all of the following may fit, so feel free to create your own mantra.

- **Success is yours:** Nobody else but you can give yourself permission to be successful in your career and life in a way that makes sense for you. You are the expert on yourself and your situation, and you are the one who is best positioned to know what will and will not work. It can make sense to take advice from those who have gone down similar paths, but integrating advice that does not support your circumstances makes no sense.

- **There is no right way:** There is no right way to be a working mother nor is there a "one size fits all" approach. Each working mother and her situation is unique. All mothers differ in terms of education, past and future careers, interest and values, and available support and resources. Do not expect to achieve the same things as someone with a different set of circumstances. It is up to you to make decisions and choices that make sense for you.

- **Compromise is crucial**: Every life stage involves compromise. Periodically review and outline your priorities for your career and your life. Recognize where you may and may not be willing to compromise, as well as what things need to change in order to achieve your life and career goals.

- **Perfect is the pits**: Striving for perfection is unrealistic. By expecting yourself to be a perfect mother, employee, daughter, and partner you will quickly learn there is no end in sight to achieving this goal. You will potentially miss opportunities to recognize what you have achieved, leaving you feeling undervalued and unfulfilled. Find joy and pleasure in what you have achieved and remember that good enough is good enough.

- **You are a role mother:** Deciding to return to paid employment or pursue a role as a stay-at-home parent is rarely an easy decision. For some, returning to work is a must. Be confident and content in your decision knowing that there are challenges and rewards to either decision you make.

Use the following area to record your working mother mantra.

My working mother mantra is _____

_____

_____

_____

CONCLUSION

We hope you enjoyed reviewing this resource as much as our team has enjoyed putting it together. We also hope that you are able to acknowledge the successes you are having in your career and in your role as a mother. We hope you are challenged and inspired to navigate your maternity leave career transition by integrating some of the strategies outlined in this resource to *Make It Work*!

Glossary

Baby blues

An experience of mood changes during the first few weeks following childbirth consisting of happiness and joy that can quickly turn to feelings of depression and sadness. Other symptoms can include irritability, restlessness, insomnia, anxiety, fatigue, poor concentration, and impatience. For symptoms that last longer than two weeks see "postpartum mood disorder."

Buddy system

Pairing women about to go on, or returning from, maternity leave with an employee who has already been through the maternity leave process and who can offer advice and support through these transitions.

Career

The sum of all the paid and unpaid roles an individual has held in his or her lifetime.

Career concepts

The modality or pattern of an individual's career decisions. Each career concept varies along three dimensions: stability, direction, and duration. Based on these dimensions, Brousseau and Driver developed four career concepts to account for how people view careers: expert, linear, spiral, and transitory.[98]

Career development

The ongoing acquisition or refinement of knowledge, skills, and abilities.

Career dialogues	Future-focused conversations that highlight career opportunities for an employee both before and after returning from her maternity leave.
Career ladder	A concept that characterizes career progression as a vertical movement.
Career lattice	The notion that career progression can be characterized by movement in several directions, including: horizontal, vertical, downward, or diagonal.
Career progression	The movement towards a particular career goal(s). These goals are determined by the individual as important and worthwhile to pursue, and may or may not include a change in title, responsibility, status, pay, flexibility, influence, etc. (also referred to as "career advancement").
Comeback coaching	Professional career transition support provided to a mother returning to work after a maternity leave or other extended leave. The coach may be an internal or external coach.
Communication plan	A plan developed in collaboration with your employer to determine how much and what type of communication you feel would be appropriate while you are on maternity leave.
Dual-career partnership	When both partners in a relationship have paid jobs outside of the home.
Employee	An individual working within an organization whose role is managed/supervised by another person or company.
Employer	An individual who holds a leadership position within an organization and is responsible for overseeing staff members. For the purposes of this guidebook, employers can include, but are not limited to, managers, supervisors, executives, and business owners.

Employment contract	An unwritten contract outlining the roles, responsibilities, and expectations of the involved parties; typically between the employer and employee (also referred to as the "psychological contract").
Exit interview	An interview conducted with an employee going on maternity leave, where the expectant mother provides feedback to improve aspects of the organization related to retention, reduced turnover, and employee development.
Expectant mothers	Mothers who, through birth or adoption, are expecting the arrival of a child.
Expert career concept	A career characterized by lifelong commitment to one profession and emphasizes the mastering of knowledge and skills in a particular field. Individuals with this career concept often value commitment, quality, security, and specialization.
Flexible hours	A schedule where an employee works a full day, but varies his or her hours, allowing flexibility at the start and end of the working day.
Flexible work arrangements	Alternative arrangements or schedules from the traditional working day and week.
Graduated return	Returning to one's regular work responsibilities after a leave, but with a gradual increase in time at work each day (or week) until the target hour is reached.
Imposter syndrome	A phenomenon that occurs when individuals are more likely to attribute their accomplishments to external factors rather than to internal factors. Consequently, the person may feel like a fraud or an imposter and as though they will soon be "outed" by others and discovered for inadequate competence and talents, which are perceived by the individual to be lacking.

Information interview	A meeting initiated with someone who is working in a career or industry of interest with the goal of furthering an understanding of the role and/or industry by gaining information and advice.
Job-sharing	An alternative work schedule where two employees voluntarily share their responsibilities, salary, benefits, and time commitments for one or more positions or sets of duties.
Limiting beliefs	Beliefs we hold that limit or constrain us in some way. These beliefs are often based on assumptions and tend to be dichotomous, using language that conveys absolutes, obligations, or limited options.
Linear career concept	A career characterized by an increased level of responsibility, influence, and status that emphasizes upward movement consistent with the idea of the career ladder. Individuals with this career concept typically value leadership, competitiveness, and achievement.
Marginalized mother	Individuals who are excluded from some or all of mainstream social, economic, cultural, or political life. Marginalized mothers most affected by maternity leave may include young mothers, first-time mothers over the age of forty, adoptive parents, aboriginal women, recently immigrated mothers, and same-sex mothers.
Maternity leave	The term inclusive of maternity, parental and adoption leave, as well as any extended care and nurturing leave following the birth or adoption of a child, taken by a new/expectant mother.
Maternity leave career transition	Changes in the new/expectant mother's employment as a result of pregnancy, birth, or adoption.
Medical leave	An absence from work, paid or unpaid, on account of an employee's temporary inability to perform duties because of sickness or disability.

Mentorship	A developmental relationship where one individual with more knowledge and experience guides the lesser experienced individual.
Mompreneur	A female business owner who actively balances the roles of mother and of entrepreneur.
Motherhood penalty	The argument that working mothers in the workplace encounter systemic disadvantages in pay, perceived competence, and benefits relative to non-parents and men.
Multi-tracking	Holding more than one paid role at the same time.
Multiple career households	Multiple income earners living under one roof.
New-concept part-time employment	Positions that offer employees a higher income and more career opportunities than traditional part-time options, resulting in enhanced prestige and job satisfaction.
New employment contract	An employment contract where employees are guaranteed employment only as they continue to add value to the organization.
Old employment Contract	An employment contract where employees are often guaranteed lifelong employment in exchange for loyalty.
Parental leave	The time away from work that a parent (mother or father) is permitted to take following the birth or adoption of a child.
Part-time work	When an individual works less than thirty hours per week.
Portfolio careers	The practice of having multiple and often varied careers as opposed to a traditional long-term, full-time position. Individuals with portfolio careers often develop a range of knowledge, skills, and experience in their diverse careers that can be applied in new settings.

Postpartum depression	Depression experienced by a mother that may start during pregnancy or at any time up to a year after the birth of a child.
Postpartum mood disorder (PPMD)	An experience of mood changes similar to the "baby blues," but that persist for longer than two weeks. Postpartum symptoms may start during pregnancy or at any time up to a year after the birth of a child.
Professional development	Encompasses all types of facilitated learning and training opportunities associated with one's career and career progression.
Psychological barriers	Cognitive or mental barriers that we have created or learned from others that prevent us from effectively reaching solutions, obtaining goals, or establishing positive relationships.
Rebranding	The act of consciously changing one's personal or career image, often precipitated by a physical, emotional, or psychological transition.
Re-onboarding	The process of re-integrating an employee returning from maternity leave into the workplace. This can include training and introducing her to any changes that have occurred during her absence.
Return to work interview	An open dialogue with your employer about any changes in roles, responsibilities, or expectations from both parties upon your return to work. This may also include a conversation about personal and career goals, challenges, and opportunities going forward.
Return to work plan	A logistical plan created between an employer and an employee returning from a maternity leave, to help transition the new mother back to work.
Sandwich generation	Individuals who are responsible for the care of family members across two or more generations.

Social media	Web sites and other forms of electronic communication that enable users to create, share, or exchange information and ideas through virtual communities and networks.
Soft return	An agreed upon start and end time where the employee may have a reduced or minimal workload the first few days or first week after her official return.
Spiral career concept	A career characterized by lateral change, typically every five to ten years. Individuals with this career concept tend to develop a much broader skill set, with each transition building upon existing skills. Individuals with this career concept typically value variety and personal growth.
Sponsorship	A workplace relationship characterized by having an ally in the organization who has the power to effect change and actively advocates for career building opportunities.
Stakeholders	Any relevant third-party who has an interest in or is otherwise impacted by your business. This can include customers, clients, co-workers, and the community.
S.T.A.R. approach	An interview technique used when answering behavioural-based questions that allows the interviewee to address information related to the situation/task, activity, and result of a requested scenario to articulate specific capabilities.
Strengths finder 360 exercise	An exercise used to create greater self-awareness whereby individuals reach out to supportive people around them to further an understanding of what others see as their strengths and gifts.
Telework	Working away from the traditional office space.
Transitory career concept	A career characterized by a high level of change. Individuals with this career concept typically value variety, independence, and flexibility.
Work-life integration	To create meaningful engagement between the interconnected roles, relationships, and responsibilities of an individual's life.

Working mother	A term used to refer to mothers who engage in paid employment, volunteer, and educational pursuits.
WORKshift	Working when and where an individual is most effective, which may include, but is not limited to, teleworking, flexible hours, and alternate scheduling.

Endnotes

1   Statistics Canada. (2014). Canadian postsecondary enrolments and graduates, 2012/2013. Retrieved from: http://www.statcan.gc.ca/daily-quotidien/141125/dq141125d-eng.htm.

2   Statistics Canada. (2010). Women in Canada: Paid Work, 1976-2009. Retrieved from: http://www.statcan.gc.ca/daily-quotidien/101209/dq101209a-eng.htm.

3   Norton, H. (2015). Why Singapore firms are increasingly hiring working mothers. HRD Singapore. Retrieved from: http://www.hrdmag.com.sg/news/why-singapore-firms-are-increasingly-hiring-working-mothers-202961.aspx.

4   Shipman, C., & Kay, K. (2009). Womenomics: Work less, achieve more, live better. New York: Harper Business.

5   Joy, L., Carter, N., Wagner, H., & Narayana, S. (2007). The Bottom Line: Corporate performance and women's representation on boards. Catalyst.

6   Desvaux, G., Devillard, S., & Sancier-Sultan, S. (2010). Women matter: Women at the top of corporations: Making it happen. McKinsey & Company.

7   Blake, R. (2006). Employee retention: What employee turnover really costs your company. Retrieved from: http://www.iwaminstitute.com/assets/files/Articles/Employee%20 Retention-What%20It%20Really%20Costs%20Your%20Company.pdf.

8   Brzezinski, M. (2015). Grow Your Value: Living and Working to Your Full Potential.

9   Owens, J. (2015). Mika Brzezinski: Value added. Working Mother. Retrieved from: http://www.workingmother.com/mika-brzezinski-value-added.

10   Kmec, J. A. (2011). Are motherhood penalties and fatherhood bonuses warranted? Comparing pro-work behaviors and conditions of mothers, fathers, and non-parents. Social Science Research, 40(2), 444-459.

11   Kmec, J. A. (2011). Are motherhood penalties and fatherhood bonuses warranted? Comparing pro-work behaviors and conditions of mothers, fathers, and non-parents. Social Science Research, 40(2), 444-459.

12   Barnett, R. C., & Hall, D. T. (2001). How to use reduced hours to win the war for talent. Organizational Dynamics, 29, 192-210.

13   Kay, K., & Shipman, C. (2014). The Confidence Code: The science and art of self-assurance-what women should know. New York: Harper Business.

14   Benko, C., Anderson, M., & Vickberg, S. (2011). The Corporate Lattice: A strategic response to the changing world of work. Deliotte University Press. Retrieved from: http://dupress.com/articles/the-corporate-lattice-rethinking-careers-in-the-changing-world-of-work/.

15   Brousseau, K. R., & Driver, M. J. (1998). Career View Concepts: Roadmaps for Career Success. Decision Dynamics Group.

16   Calgary Career Counselling. (2012). Connecting the Pieces: A Workbook for Creating Your Ideal Career.

17   Simonsen, P. (1997). Promoting a Development Culture in Your Organization: Using Career Development as a Change Agent. Davies-Black Publishing, Mountain View.

18   Statistics Canada. (2015). Insights on Canadian Society – Employment Patterns of Families with Children. Statistics Canada Publication No. 75-006-X; ISN 2291-0840; Author: Sharanjit Uppal).

19   Neault, R., & Pickerell, D. (2005). Dual-career couples: The juggling act. Canadian Journal of Counselling, Vol 39, 3.

20   Neault, R., & Pickerell, D. (2005). Dual-career couples: The juggling act. Canadian Journal of Counselling, Vol 39, 3.

21   Braverman, B. (2015). How to make multi-generational housing work for your family. Forbes. Retrieved from: http://www.forbes.com/sites/bethbraverman/2015/06/18/ how-to-make-multi-generational-housing-work-for-your-family/#42150f3821f7.

22   Braverman, B. (2015). How to make multi-generational housing work for your family. Forbes. Retrieved from: http://www.forbes.com/sites/bethbraverman/2015/06/18/ how-to-make-multi-generational-housing-work-for-your-family/#42150f3821f7.

23   Braverman, B. (2015). How to make multi-generational housing work for your family. Forbes. Retrieved from: http://www.forbes.com/sites/bethbraverman/2015/06/18/ how-to-make-multi-generational-housing-work-for-your-family/#42150f3821f7.

24   Ferrao, V. (2009). Women in Canada: A gender-based statistical report. Statistics Canada. Retrieved from: http://www.statcan.gc.ca/pub/89-503-x/2010001/ article/11387-eng.htm.

25   Mathison, D., & Finney, M.I. (2009). Unlock the Hidden Job Market: 6 Steps to a Successful Job Search When Times are Tough. Pearson Education Inc., Publishing as FT Press, New Jersey.

26   Bridges, W. (2004). Transitions: Making sense of life's change. Da Capo Press, Cambridge MA.

27   Tahirkheli, N. N., Cherry, A. S., Tackett, A. P., McCaffree, M., & Gillaspy, S. R. (2014). Postpartum depression on the neonatal intensive care unit: Current perspectives. International Journal of Women's Health, 6, 975-987. doi: 10.2147/IJWH.S54666.

28   Canadian Mental Health Association. (2015). Postpartum Depression. Retrieved from: https://www.cmha.bc.ca/get-informed/mental-health-information/ postpartum-depression.

29   Burgess, N. (2013). The motherhood penalty: How gender and parental status influence judgments of job-related competence and organizational commitment. Schmidt Labor Research Center Seminar Paper Series, University of Rhode Island.

30   Burgess, N. (2013). The motherhood penalty: How gender and parental status influence judgments of job-related competence and organizational commitment. Schmidt Labor Research Center Seminar Paper Series, University of Rhode Island.

31   Mattam, L., & Seth, R. (2014). Mom's the word: How organizations can change the impact of motherhood on long-term career success. The Mattam Group, Toronto, Ontario.

32   Mattam, L., & Seth, R. (2014). Mom's the word: How organizations can change the impact of motherhood on long-term career success. The Mattam Group, Toronto, Ontario.

33   Morin, A. (2014). The five things successful parents give up to reach a work-life balance. Forbes. Retrieved from: http://www.forbes.com/sites/amymorin/2014/01/20/the-five-things-successful-working-parents-give-up-to-reach-a-work-life-balance/2/.

34   Kmec, J. A. (2011). Are motherhood penalties and fatherhood bonuses warranted? Comparing pro-work behaviors and conditions of mothers, fathers, and non-parents. Social Science Research, 40(2), 444-459.

35   Poduval, J., & Poduval, M. (2009). Working mothers: How much working, how much mothers, and where is the womanhood? Mens Sana Monograph, 7(1), 63-79.

36   Kmec, J. A. (2011). Are motherhood penalties and fatherhood bonuses warranted? Comparing pro-work behaviors and conditions of mothers, fathers, and non-parents. Social Science Research, 40(2), 444-459.

37   Correll, S.J., Benard, S., & Paik, I. (2007). Getting a Job: Is There a Motherhood Penalty? American Journal of Sociology, 112(5), 1297-1339.

38   Mattam, L., & Seth, R. (2014). Mom's the word: How organizations can change the impact of motherhood on long-term career success. The Mattam Group, Toronto, Ontario.

39   Haddock, S. A., Ziemba, S. J., Zimmerman, T. S., & Current, L. R. (2001). Ten adaptive strategies for family and work balance: Advice from successful families. Journal of Marital and Family Therapy, 27(4), 445-458.

40   Galinsky, E. (1999). Ask the children: What America's children really think about working parents. William Morrow and Company, Inc., New York, New York.

41   Galinsky, E. (1999). Ask the children: What America's children really think about working parents. William Morrow and Company, Inc., New York, New York.

42   U.S. Department of Health and Human Services. (2006). The NICHD Study of Early Child Care and Youth Development. Retrieved from National Institute of Child Health and Human Development: https://www.nichd.nih.gov/publications/pubs/documents/seccyd_06.pdf.

43   National American Agreement on Labor Cooperation. (no date). Women's Guide to Pregnancy on the Job in Canada. Washington, Connecticut. Retrieved from: http://www.naalc.org/index.cfm?page=827.

44   Ontario Human Rights Commission. (no date). Policy on preventing discrimination because of pregnancy and breastfeeding. Toronto, Ontario. Retrieved from: http://www.ohrc.on.ca/en/policy-preventing-discrimination-because-pregnancy-and-breastfeeding/7-employment.

45   Government of Alberta. (2014). Maternity Leave and Parental Leave. Employment Standards: Rights and responsibilities at work.

46   Government of Alberta. (2014). Maternity Leave and Parental Leave. Employment Standards: Rights and responsibilities at work.

47   Government of Alberta. (2014). Maternity Leave and Parental Leave. Employment Standards: Rights and responsibilities at work.

48   Ontario Human Rights Commission. (no date). Policy on preventing discrimination because of pregnancy and breastfeeding. Toronto, Ontario. Retrieved from: http://www.ohrc.on.ca/en/policy-preventing-discrimination-because-pregnancy-and-breastfeeding/7-employment.

49   Ontario Human Rights Commission. (no date). Policy on preventing discrimination because of pregnancy and breastfeeding. Toronto, Ontario. Retrieved from: http://www.ohrc.on.ca/en/policy-preventing-discrimination-because-pregnancy-and-breastfeeding/7-employment.

50   Canadian Human Rights Commission. (no date). Policy on Pregnancy & Human Rights in the Workplace. Retrieved from: http://www.chrc-ccdp.gc.ca/eng/content/policy-and-best-practices-page-2.

51   Ontario Human Rights Commission. (no date). Policy on preventing discrimination because of pregnancy and breastfeeding. Toronto, Ontario. Retrieved from:

http://www.ohrc.on.ca/en/policy-preventing-discrimination-because-pregnancy-and-breastfeeding/7-employment.

52   Commission for Labor Cooperation. Women's guide to pregnancy on the job. Retrieved from: http://www.naalc.org/.

53   Kay, K., & Shipman, C. (2014). The Confidence Code: The science and art of self-assurance-what women should know. New York: Harper Business.

54   Cuddy, A. (no date). Your body language shapes who you are. TED Talk. Retrieved from: https://www.ted.com/talks/amy_cuddy_your_body_language_shapes_who_you_are.

55   Behavioral Science Guys. (no date). One Simple Skill to Curb Unconscious Gender Bias. YouTube Video. Retrieved from: https://www.youtube.com/watch?v=SEHi4yauhu8.

56   Hewlett, S.A. (2013). The right way to find a career sponsor. Harvard Business Review. Retrieved from: https://hbr.org/2013/09/the-right-way-to-find-a-career-sponsor/.

57   Hewlett, S.A. (2013). The right way to find a career sponsor. Harvard Business Review. Retrieved from: https://hbr.org/2013/09/the-right-way-to-find-a-career-sponsor/.

58   Catalyst. (2011). Fostering sponsorship success among high performers and leaders. Retrieved from: http://www.catalyst.org/knowledge/fostering-sponsorship-success-among-high-performers-and-leaders.

Foust-Cummings, H., Dinolfo, S., & Kohler, J. (2011). Sponsoring women to success. Catalyst. Retrieved from: http://www.catalyst.org/publication/485/23/sponsoring-women-to-success.

59   Catalyst. (2011). Fostering sponsorship success among high performers and leaders. Retrieved from: http://www.catalyst.org/knowledge/fostering-sponsorship-success-among-high-performers-and-leaders.

Foust-Cummings, H., Dinolfo, S., & Kohler, J. (2011). Sponsoring women to success. Catalyst. Retrieved from: http://www.catalyst.org/publication/485/23/sponsoring-women-to-success.

60   Fudge, J. (2006). Control Over Working Time and Work-Life Balance: A Detailed Analysis of the Canada Labour Code, Part III. Human Resources and Skills

Development Canada. Retrieved from: http://www.hrsdc.gc.ca/eng/labour/employ-ment_standards/fls/pdf/research17.pdf.

61   Working Families. (2011). Discover the benefits of job sharing. Article id: 3568. Retrieved from: http://www.acas.org.uk/index.aspx.

62   Katepoo, P. (2015). Four compelling employer advantages of job sharing. Retrieved from: http://www.workoptions.com/job-sharing-advantages.

63   Gallo, A. (September 2013). How to make a job sharing situation work. Harvard Business Review. Retrieved from: https://hbr.org/2013/09/how-to-make-a-job-sharing-situation-work/.

64   Moran, G. (2015). Could sharing your job be the solution to burnout? Fast Company. Retrieved from: http://www.fastcompany.com/3047108/how-to-be-a-success-at-everything/how-sharing-your-job-might-be-the-solution-to-burn-out.

65   Grzywacz, J. G., Carlson, D. W., & Shulkin, S. (2008). Schedule flexibility and stress: Linking formal flexible arrangements and perceived flexibility to employee health. Community, Work & Family, 11(2), 199-214.

66   Statistics Canada. (2010). Classification of full-time and part-time work hours. Retrieved from: http://www.statcan.gc.ca/eng/concepts/definitions/labour-class03b.

67   Williams, J.C., Manwell, J., & Bornstein, S. (2006). "Opt Out" or Pushed Out? How the Press Covers Work/Family Conflict. The Centre for Work-Life Law. Retrieved from: http://www.worklifelaw.org/pubs/OptOutPushedOut.pdf.

68   Hill, E.J., & Kadi, V. (2001). Beyond the mommy track: The influence of a reduced-hours work schedule program on the work/life balance of professional women. Paper presented at the 63rd Annual Conference of the National Council on Family Relations, Rochester, NY.

       Hill, E.J., Martinson, V., & Ferris, M. (2004). New-concept part-time employment as a work-family adaptive strategy for women. Family Relations, 53, 282-292.

69   WORKshift. (2015). Environmental benefits of WORKshift. Retrieved from: http://www.workshiftcanada.com/workshift-planet/benefits.

70   WORKshift. (2015). Environmental benefits of WORKshift.Retrieved from: http://www.workshiftcanada.com/workshift-planet/benefits.

71   Industry Canada. (2006). Sustaining the momentum: An economic forum on women entrepreneurs. Catalogue Number 54357E. Retrieved from: http://publications.gc.ca/site/eng/290660/publication.html.

72   Leblanc, H. (2015). The economic leadership and prosperity of Canadian women. House of Commons of Canada, Ottawa, ON.

73   Monosoff, T. (2005). The Mom Inventors Handbook. McGraw-Hill Education, New York, NY.

74   Monosoff, T. (2005). The Mom Inventors Handbook. McGraw-Hill Education, New York, NY.

75   Patterson, N., & Mavin, S. (2009). Women entrepreneurs: Jumping the corporate ship and gaining new wings. International Small Business Journal, 27, 173-192.

76   Richomme-Huet, K., & Vial, V. (2014). Business Lessons from a "Mompreneurs" Network. Global Business and Organizational Excellence, 33, 18-27.

77   Humbert, A. L., & Lewis, S. (2008). "I have No Life Other than Work" – Long Working Hours, Blurred Boundaries, and Family Life: The Case of Irish Entrepreneurs. In Burke, R.J., & Cooper, C.L. (Eds.), The Long Work Hours Culture: Causes, Consequences and Choices, Emerald, Bigley, UK, 59-181.

78   Bechthold, K. (2010). The Entrepreneurial Mom's Guide to Running Your Own Business. Self-Counsel Press, Vancouver, BC.

79   Ballon, A., & Botterell, D. (2011). Mom Inc.: Raising your family and your business without losing your mind or your shirt. HarperCollins, Toronto, ON.

80   Neault, R., & Pickerell, D. (2011). Look Before You Leap: Self-Employment Survival Strategies. CERIC, Aldergrove, BC.

81   DeVito, J. (2010). How adolescent mothers feel about becoming a parent. Journal of Perinatal Education, 19(2), 25–34.

82   Clemmens, D. (2001). The relationship between social support and adolescent mothers' interactions with their infants: A meta-analysis. Journal of Obstetric, Gynecologic, and Neonatal Nursing, 30(4), 410–420.

Clemmens, D. (2003). Adolescent motherhood: A meta-analysis of qualitative studies. MCN. The American Journal of Maternal Child Nursing, 28(2), 93–99.

Gee, C., & Rhodes, J. (2003). Adolescent mothers' relationship with their children's biological fathers: Social support, social strain, and relationship continuity. Journal of Family Psychology, 17(3), 370–383.

Rentschler, D. (2003). Pregnant adolescent's perspectives of pregnancy. The American Journal of Maternal Child Nursing, 28(6), 377–383.

83   DeVito, J. (2007). Self-perceptions of parenting among adolescent mothers. The Journal of Perinatal Education, 16(1), 16–23.

84   Statistics Canada (2008). The Children of Older First-Time Mothers in Canada: Their Health and Development. Statistics Canada Catalogue No. 89-599-M).

85   Laughlin, L. (2011). Maternity leave and employment patterns of first-time mothers: 1961 – 2008. Household Economic Studies, 2–21.

86   Silver, Cynthia. (2000). Being there: The time dual-earner couples spend with their children. Canadian Social Trends (Statistics Canada Publication No. 11-008-XPE) 57 (summer): 26-29.

87   Ward, R., & Spitze, G. (1998). Sandwiched marriages: The implications of child and parent relations for marital quality in midlife. Social Forces, 77(2), 647-666.

Marks, N.F. (1998). Does it hurt to care? Caregiving, work-family conflict and midlife well-being. Journal of Marriage and the Family, 60(4), 951-966.

88   Williams, C. (2004). The Sandwich Generation. Statistics Canada Publication No. 75-001-XIE.

89   Williams, C. (2004). The Sandwich Generation. Statistics Canada Publication No. 75-001-XIE.

90   Paul-Carson, P. (2011). Employment insurance benefits for adoptive parents. Adoption Council of Canada. Retrieved from: http://www.adoption.ca/ei-benefits-for-adoptive-parents.

91   Higginbottom, G., Bell, A.S., Arsenault, J., & Pillay, J. (2012). An integrative review of experiences of maternity services for immigrant women in Canada. Diversity and Equality in Health and Care, 9, 253–266.

92   Kaczorowski, J., O'Brien, B., & Lily Lee, B. N. (2011). Comparison of maternity experiences of Canadian-born and recent and non-recent immigrant women: findings from the Canadian Maternity Experiences Survey. J Obstet Gynaecol Can, 33(11), 1105-1115.

93   Reitmanova, S., & Gustafson, D. L. (2008). "They can't understand it": maternity health and care needs of immigrant Muslim women in St. John's, Newfoundland. Maternal and Child Health Journal, 12(1), 101-111.

94   Sword, W., Watt, S., & Krueger, P. (2006). Postpartum health, service needs, and access to care experiences of immigrant and Canadian-born women. Journal of Obstetric, Gynecologic and Neonatal Nursing, 35(6), 717-727.

95   Hancock, H. (2006). Aboriginal women's perinatal needs, experiences, and maternity services: A literature review to enable considerations to be made about quality indicators. Ngaanyatjarra Health Service (ISBN: 978-0-646-47273-7).

96   Linville, D., & O'Neil, M. (no date). Same-sex parents and their children – AAMFT therapy topics. Retrieved from: http://www.aamft.org/imis15/aamft/Content/Consumer_Updates/Same-sex_Parents_and_Their_Children.aspx.

97   Linville, D., & O'Neil, M. (no date). Same-sex parents and their children – AAMFT therapy topics. Retrieved from: http://www.aamft.org/imis15/aamft/Content/Consumer_Updates/Same-sex_Parents_and_Their_Children.aspx.

98   Brousseau, K. R., & Driver, M. J. (1998). Career View Concepts: Roadmaps for Career Success. Decision Dynamics Group.

www.ingramcontent.com/pod-product-compliance
Lightning Source LLC
Chambersburg PA
CBHW052342210326
41597CB00037B/6230